SUMMARY OF DIVINE ENCOUNTERS

Your Invitation to Experiential Knowledge of the Living God

PAUL MANWARING

BILL JOHNSON

D DESTINY IMAGE

Destiny Image P.O. Box 310, Shippensburg, PA 17257-0310

This book and all other Destiny Image's books are available at Christian bookstores and distributors worldwide.

For Worldwide Distribution.

Reach us on the Internet: www.destinyimage.com.

ISBN 13 TP: 9780768484199

ISBN 13 eBook: 9780768484205

CONTENTS

INTRODUCTION

❧

INTRODUCTION TO THE SUMMARY OF
DIVINE ENCOUNTERS

In *Divine Encounters*, the theme of transformation through personal experiences with God is explored in depth, emphasizing the profound impact these encounters have on the believer's life. From the moment of conversion to the ongoing process of spiritual growth, encounters with God are not just fleeting emotional experiences but powerful catalysts for change, purpose, and mission. Through biblical examples such as Paul's dramatic encounter on the road to Damascus, this book highlights how ordinary people are forever changed when they meet the living God. These moments become the foundation for understanding the gospel, shaping the believer's calling, and equipping them for their God-given purpose.

Each chapter of this summary dives into the heart of these divine encounters, showing how God interacts with His people through personal, life-changing moments. Encounters are presented as both an invitation and a challenge—to not only experience God's presence but to allow it to transform every aspect of life. This transformation brings about a new sense of identity, a deeper understanding of scripture, and a clearer path toward fulfilling one's destiny in Christ.

The book also emphasizes that these divine encounters are not confined to a select few; they are accessible to all who seek God with an open and surrendered heart. As readers journey through the summary, they are encouraged to recognize the significance of their own encounters with God, to pursue more of His presence, and to understand how these moments fit into the larger narrative of their spiritual life and calling.

Ultimately, *Divine Encounters* serves as both an inspiration and a guide, showing readers how to integrate their encounters with God into their daily lives, how to steward these moments well, and how to allow them to shape the future direction of their faith. Through this summary, readers will gain practical insights into the power of divine encounters, while being invited to seek and expect more of God's transformative presence in their own lives.

CHAPTER 1

THE VALUE OF
EXPERIENCE

Bible Verse

Ephesians 3:17-19 (NASB95) - "So that Christ may
dwell in your hearts through faith; and that you,
being rooted and grounded in love, may be able to
comprehend with all the saints what is the breadth
and length and height and depth, and to know the
love of Christ which surpasses knowledge, that you
may be filled up to all the fullness of God."

Introduction

Bill Johnson uses his personal experiences,
particularly from his marriage, to illuminate
the transformative power of shared life experiences and encounters with God. He emphasizes that true relationship—whether with people
or with God—thrives on meaningful experiences
that foster growth and deepen trust.

Word of Wisdom

"He who has an experience is never at

the mercy of those with an argument." -
Bill Johnson

Main Theme

The chapter delves into the pivotal role of experiences in shaping our faith and our lives, arguing that encounters with God are not anomalies but essential elements of a vibrant spiritual life.

Key Points

- Experiences are foundational to relationships, not only enriching marriages but also our relationship with God.
- The Bible is filled with narratives of divine encounters, challenging our perceptions of what is normal.
- Encounters with God should not be dismissed as outliers; they are vital to our spiritual understanding and growth.
- True encounters with God involve transformation across all aspects of life: physical, emotional, and spiritual.
- Experiences with God challenge our limitations and expand our horizons beyond human comprehension.
- Our response to divine encounters should be one of surrender, letting them reshape our lives and beliefs.

Key Themes

- **Relational Foundation of Experiences:** Johnson highlights that relationships, particularly marriage, are built on the accumulation of shared experiences. These experiences deepen intimacy and understanding, similar to how our spiritual encounters with God enhance our relationship with Him.
- **Biblical Precedent for Divine Encounters:** The text draws parallels between personal stories and biblical accounts like those of Ezekiel, Daniel, and Saul, demonstrating that extraordinary encounters with God are scripturally sound and historically significant in shaping faith.
- **Impact of Experiences on Perception:** Experiences, especially with the divine, shift our perceptions of possibility and normality. Johnson argues that what is considered an outlier in one context may be a foretaste of a new normal in another, particularly in spiritual matters.
- **Transformation Through Encounters:** Johnson emphasizes that encounters with God are transformative, affecting not just one area but every facet of a person's life. He uses the healing of the lame man in Acts 3 as a vivid example of holistic healing—body, soul, and spirit.
- **The Role of Surrender in Experiences:** Following a divine encounter, the challenge often lies in our response—whether we allow the experience to change us or resist its

3

implications. Johnson uses King Saul as a cautionary tale of the latter, underscoring the need for surrender to God's transformative work.

Conclusion

Bill Johnson's chapter challenges readers to embrace and seek divine encounters, positioning them not as rare spiritual anomalies but as normative, transformative experiences that align us more closely with God's purposes. These encounters offer a fuller understanding of God's dimensions of love and power, inviting believers to step beyond intellectual faith into experiential knowledge that shapes their entire being.

CHAPTER 2

ONE DIVINE MOMENT

Bible Verse

Acts 9:5 (NIV) - "'Who are you, Lord?' Saul asked. 'I am Jesus, whom you are persecuting,' he replied."

Introduction

This chapter captures the dramatic transformation of Saul on the road to Damascus through a journalistic lens, vividly recounting the moment Saul's life was irrevocably changed by an encounter with Jesus Christ. It underscores the profound impact of divine moments that alter the course of history and personal destinies.

Word of Wisdom

"Those who meet Jesus are left with a choice to follow or deny." - Paul Manwaring

. . .

Main Theme

The focus of this chapter is the transformative power of divine encounters, exemplified by Saul's conversion, which not only altered his own trajectory but also had a ripple effect on Christian history.

Key Points

- Saul, once a persecutor of Christians, experienced a radical transformation following a divine encounter with Jesus.
- This encounter was so powerful that it not only stopped Saul in his tracks but also blinded him, symbolizing his profound spiritual awakening.
- Ananias, despite knowing Saul's reputation, played a crucial role in Saul's baptism and receipt of the Holy Spirit.
- Following his conversion, Saul began to preach fervently about Jesus, indicating a complete reversal of his prior beliefs and actions.
- Saul's story is a prime example of how a single moment can redefine a person's life and beliefs.
- The skepticism and challenges Saul faced post-conversion illustrate the societal impact and controversy surrounding such transformative experiences.

Key Themes

- **Journalistic Perspective on Divine Encounters:** This narrative technique highlights the immediacy and dramatic nature of Saul's transformation, presenting it as breaking news that captivates the reader's attention and underscores the historical significance of the event.
- **Symbolism of Saul's Blindness:** Saul's physical blindness serves as a metaphor for his spiritual enlightenment. The restoration of his sight parallels his newfound spiritual vision, marking his total transformation from a persecutor of Christians to a proponent of Christ.
- **Role of Ananias in Saul's Transformation:** Ananias embodies the courage and obedience that are often required in divine plans. His interaction with Saul highlights the themes of grace and redemption, showing that anyone, regardless of their past, can be used mightily by God.
- **Impact of Saul's Conversion on His Preaching:** Saul's immediate shift to preaching the gospel powerfully illustrates the authenticity and depth of his encounter with Jesus. It also shows how personal experiences with divinity can lead to public declarations of faith and shifts in religious paradigms.
- **Social and Religious Repercussions:** Saul's story reflects the broader implications of personal spiritual experiences on society and religious

communities. His acceptance by other Christians, despite initial skepticism, underscores themes of forgiveness, community, and the challenging of religious norms.

Conclusion

The chapter vividly illustrates how divine encounters, such as Saul's conversion, are not just personal moments but pivotal events that have the power to transform beliefs and influence religious history. Saul's journey from persecution to proclamation serves as a profound example of the unexpected and life-changing encounters with the divine that challenge and redefine our understanding of faith and purpose.

CHAPTER 3

ENCOUNTERS

Bible Verse

Colossians 2:10 (NASB95) - "And in Him you have been made complete, and he is the head over all rule and authority."

Introduction

Paul Manwaring discusses the evolution and significance of the term "encounter" in Christian discourse, emphasizing its profound implications for personal faith and transformation, particularly highlighted by experiences such as the Toronto Blessing.

Word of Wisdom

"They are only one encounter away from it." - This highlights the transformative power of a single divine encounter, as discussed by Paul Manwaring.

Main Theme

The chapter explores the concept of divine encounters as transformative events that redefine one's faith journey, drawing a parallel between personal spiritual experiences and biblical accounts such as Saul's conversion.

Key Points

- "Encounter" has become a key term in Christianity, especially since the 1990s, symbolizing direct experiences with God.
- An encounter with God is transformative, making profound changes in one's spiritual and everyday life.
- Saul's conversion on the Damascus Road is presented as a quintessential example of a life-altering divine encounter.
- Divine encounters are not only personal but also have communal and historical significance, impacting broader Christian thought.
- The chapter advocates for a balanced view of encounters, recognizing both monumental and simple experiences as valid.
- Manwaring calls for an accessible, inclusive Christianity that emphasizes continuous and transformative encounters with God.

Key Themes

- **Transformation Beyond Language:**
  The chapter critiques the commodification

of spiritual language, particularly the term "encounter," urging Christians to ensure these terms remain deeply connected to genuine faith experiences rather than becoming mere jargon.

- **Historical and Personal Significance of Encounters:** It connects historical revivals and personal transformations, illustrating how pivotal moments like Saul's conversion are not only scripturally significant but also serve as metaphors for personal spiritual awakenings today.

- **Encounters as a Process, Not a Destination:** Encounters are described as ongoing processes that affect one's spiritual journey continuously; they are not one-time events but gateways to deeper faith and transformation.

- **Inclusivity and Accessibility in Spiritual Experiences:** Manwaring emphasizes that encounters with God should be accessible to all believers, regardless of their spiritual maturity or life circumstances, advocating for a faith that is as inclusive as it is transformative.

- **The Practical Impact of Divine Encounters:** The narrative discusses how encounters should lead to practical changes in behavior and outlook, much like encountering a wild animal changes how one navigates their path, suggesting that true spiritual encounters compel a reevaluation and alteration of one's life path.

Conclusion

"Encounters" by Paul Manwaring serves as a compelling call to recognize and seek divine encounters that not only promise personal transformation but also empower individuals to live out a faith that is active, inclusive, and continuously evolving. The chapter invites readers to view their spiritual experiences as part of a larger divine narrative, encouraging a life of constant seeking and responsiveness to God's presence.

CHAPTER 4

SAUL OF TARSUS

Bible Verse

"And in Him you have been made complete, and
He is the head over all rule and authority." -
Colossians 2:10 (NASB95)

Introduction

Paul Manwaring explores the profound and
transformational encounter of Saul of
Tarsus on the road to Damascus. This
chapter delves into the historical and religious significance of Saul's conversion, not merely as a
change of faith but as a pivotal moment of divine
intervention that redefined his identity and
mission.

Word of Wisdom

*"They are only one encounter away
from it." - This statement highlights the
potential of a single divine encounter to*

radically transform a life, as it did for Saul.

Main Theme

The chapter focuses on the transformative encounter of Saul with Christ, which not only converted him from a persecutor of Christians to a devoted apostle but also marked a significant completion of his faith journey.

Key Points

- Saul's experience on the Damascus road is one of the Bible's most dramatic narratives, symbolizing profound transformation.
- Saul met Jesus Christ in a life-altering moment that redirected his entire purpose and identity.
- Prior to his conversion, Saul was a Pharisee with strong credentials, deeply embedded in religious traditions.
- His encounter was not just a conversion but a completion, integrating his past with his new mission in Christ.
- This encounter led Saul, who became Paul, to a mission that would define Christian theology.
- Paul's writings are foundational to Christian doctrine, reflecting the depth of his transformation and understanding of faith.

Key Themes

- **The Complexity of Saul's Identity:**
Saul's rich and varied identity as a Hebrew,
Israelite, and Pharisee is crucial to
understanding the depth of his conversion.
His background positioned him uniquely
to bridge diverse cultures and religious
traditions, making his teachings
particularly impactful.
- **The Impact of Saul's Conversion:**
Saul's conversion was not merely a personal
transformation but a pivotal event for
Christianity. It shifted his zeal from
persecuting Christians to spreading the
Christian faith, highlighting the power of
divine intervention.
- **The Theological Implications of the
Encounter:** Saul's encounter with Christ
on the Damascus road goes beyond a mere
biblical story; it is a theological anchor in
Christian teachings, emphasizing the
transformative power of direct encounters
with God.
- **Narrative Consistency and Changes:**
The recounting of Saul's conversion in Acts
illustrates the consistency of his testimony
and the changes in his understanding and
expression of his faith over time.
- **Life as a Reflection of Divine
Purpose:** Saul's life post-conversion
reflects a journey of continual encounters
with God, demonstrating that each
believer's life can be a testament to God's
ongoing work and purpose.

Conclusion

Paul Manwaring's exploration of Saul of Tarsus invites readers to see beyond the familiar narrative to the profound theological and personal changes that defined one of Christianity's most influential figures. It underscores that encounters with the divine are not only foundational to faith but are also ongoing opportunities for transformation and growth.

CHAPTER 5

AN INTRODUCTION TO PAUL'S WRITINGS

Bible Verse

"For what the Law could not do, weak as it was through the flesh, God did: sending His own Son in the likeness of sinful flesh and as an offering for sin." - Romans 8:3 (NASB)

Introduction

Paul Manwaring delves into how the dramatic encounter of Saul on the road to Damascus profoundly influenced all of Paul's subsequent writings. This chapter explores the intertwining of Paul's theological insights with his transformative encounter, suggesting that his writings cannot be fully understood without recognizing the impact of this experience.

Word of Wisdom

"Our theology begins with a creator God who wanted to be with us." - This encapsulates the foundational belief that

divine encounters are integral to understanding and experiencing God. Paul Manwaring

Main Theme

The chapter examines how Paul's writings are imbued with the insights and revelations from his encounter with the resurrected Jesus, fundamentally shaping his theological framework and his presentation of the gospel.

Key Points

- Paul's theology was profoundly influenced by his personal encounter with Jesus, shaping all his future writings.
- He spent years pondering his encounter, which deeply informed his theological outlook.
- Paul's letters integrate his experiences with robust theological discourse, moving beyond intellectual study to personal testimony.
- His writings frequently reference his conversion experience, using it as a foundation to explore and explain deeper theological truths.
- Paul's approach to theology was experiential, emphasizing a living and dynamic encounter with God.
- His interpretation of scripture was revolutionary, presenting Jesus as the

fulfillment of the Old Testament and the embodiment of the New Covenant.

Key Themes

- **The Impact of Encounter on Theology:** Paul's encounter with Jesus was not just a moment of conversion but a profound theological revelation that continued to influence all his writings. His deep engagement with his own transformative experience allowed him to present a theology that was both deeply personal and universally applicable.
- **Paul's Use of the Old Testament:** Paul's extensive knowledge of the Old Testament and his transformative encounter with Jesus allowed him to bridge the Old and New Testaments. He demonstrated how Christ fulfilled Old Testament prophecies, providing a richer understanding of scripture.
- **Intellectual Understanding vs. Experiential Encounter:** Studying Paul's letters through the lens of his encounter reveals the limitations of purely intellectual approaches to theology. Paul's writings challenge readers to seek their own divine encounters, emphasizing that true understanding comes through personal experience with the divine.
- **Legalism vs. Encounter:** Paul's teachings counter legalistic interpretations of scripture

by emphasizing the role of divine encounters in understanding and living out the gospel. His writings advocate for a relationship with God that is marked by ongoing encounters rather than adherence to legalistic norms.

- **Continuity and Completion in Paul's Theology:** Paul saw his encounter as both a continuation of his religious heritage and a radical completion of it. His theology does not discard his past but uses it as a foundation to reveal the comprehensive and transformative nature of the gospel.

Conclusion

Paul Manwaring's exploration of Paul's writings through the prism of his Damascus road encounter offers a profound insight into how personal experiences with the divine can deeply influence theological insight and expression. This approach invites believers to not only study scripture but to seek personal encounters with God that illuminate and transform their understanding, similar to how Paul's own encounter profoundly shaped his life and letters.

CHAPTER 6

GRACE

Bible Verse

"For by grace you have been saved through faith...
not a result of works, so that no one may boast." -
Ephesians 2:8-9 (NASB)

Introduction

This chapter explores the profound influence of grace in Paul's life and writings, particularly following his transformative encounter on the road to Damascus. Paul's experience illustrates the deeply personal and life-altering nature of grace, which he articulates in his epistles.

Word of Wisdom

"Grace transformed him. Grace empowered him. Grace, in many respects, defined him." - This captures the essence

of grace's transformative power in Paul's life. Paul Manwaring

Main Theme

The theme focuses on understanding grace not just as a theological concept but as a dynamic and transformative experience, illustrated vividly through Paul's life and his writings.

Key Points

- Paul's writings on grace are deeply rooted in his personal encounter with Jesus, reflecting a profound understanding of grace's transformative power.
- Grace is portrayed as a spontaneous, unmerited divine favor that is both salvific and sanctifying.
- Paul's descriptions of grace emphasize its role in empowerment and ongoing spiritual growth, beyond mere salvation.
- The chapter critiques the dilution of the concept of grace in modern Christian discourse, urging a deeper, more biblically rooted understanding.
- Paul's use of grace in his letters is extensive, suggesting it as a central theme that influenced his theological and practical teachings.
- The encounter with grace on the Damascus road is presented as a foundational moment that shaped Paul's entire ministry and message.

Key Themes

- **Grace as Encounter and Transformation:** Paul's encounter with grace was not merely a moment of theological insight but a profound transformation that redirected his life's purpose. This transformation through grace is a central theme in his writings, where he emphasizes that grace is an encounter with the divine that reshapes one's identity and mission.

- **Grace Beyond Salvation:** While grace is foundational to salvation, its role extends into every aspect of Christian living, empowering believers in their spiritual growth and practical life. Paul's teachings explore how grace equips and empowers believers to overcome weaknesses and manifest God's power in their lives.

- **Historical and Theological Context of Grace:** Paul's understanding of grace was revolutionary in the context of Jewish and Roman religious practices of his time, which were often works-based. His letters argue for a grace that is unearned and sufficient, countering both legalism and moralism.

- **Practical Implications of Grace:** Through his letters, Paul shows that grace should lead to a life of humility, service, and a departure from old ways of living. He emphasizes that grace brings about an ethical transformation that aligns believers' lives with the teachings of Jesus.

- **Continual Relevance of Grace:** The chapter encourages believers to seek a personal and ongoing experience of grace, similar to Paul's, which continually redefines and empowers their faith journey. It stresses that grace is not a one-time event but a continuous source of strength and renewal.

Conclusion

"Grace" in Paul's context is explored as a dynamic and transformative force, pivotal not only for understanding salvation but for fostering continuous spiritual growth and empowerment. The chapter urges believers to embrace a deeper, experiential understanding of grace, reflecting on its impact in Paul's life as a template for Christian living and ministry. This approach challenges superficial interpretations of grace, advocating for a return to a biblically grounded, experiential understanding that transforms lives.

CHAPTER 7

NO CONDEMNATION

Bible Verse

"There is therefore now no condemnation to those who are in Christ Jesus." - Romans 8:1 (NKJV)

Introduction

This chapter delves into the profound impact of Paul's encounter with Jesus on the road to Damascus, particularly focusing on the theme of condemnation—or rather, the absence of it—which Paul famously discusses in his letter to the Romans.

Word of Wisdom

"Saul the condemner, who without intervention would have been the condemned, wrote to the Romans: 'There is therefore now no condemnation to those who are in Christ Jesus'." - This state-

ment captures the transformative revelation Paul received about divine grace and judgment.

Main Theme

The theme centers on the transformative grace that redefines judgement and condemnation, as experienced by Paul during his encounter with Jesus, shaping his understanding and teachings on divine justice and mercy.

Key Points

• Paul's encounter with Jesus was devoid of condemnation despite his past actions.

• His experience redefined his understanding of justice, emphasizing grace and redemption.

• The encounter parallels the biblical story of the prodigal son, symbolizing divine acceptance.

• Paul's writings frequently revisit the theme of grace over condemnation.

• His teachings advocate for a life free from shame and condemnation for all believers.

• Paul viewed his transformative encounter as a pivotal moment that aligned him with God's righteousness through faith.

Key Themes

• **Grace Over Condemnation:** The encounter with Jesus introduced Paul to a system of grace that stands in contrast to the condemnation he had anticipated. This grace is a recurring theme in his writings, where he underscores the absence of condemnation for those in Christ, reshaping how believers understand their relationship with divine justice.

- **Empowerment Through Grace:** Paul's teachings emphasize that grace empowers believers to live free of shame and condemnation. He uses his own experience as a testament to the power of grace to erase the deepest stains of the past, offering new life and a new identity rooted in Christ's redemptive work.

- **Theological Reinterpretation of Justice:** Paul reinterprets divine justice through the lens of his encounter, advocating a theology that celebrates redemption over retribution. His letters encourage believers to embrace a view of God as a redeemer rather than a condemner.

- **Practical Implications of No Condemnation:** By declaring "no condemnation," Paul sets forth a practical framework for Christian living that rejects shame and embraces faith-driven righteousness. This approach not only impacts personal spirituality but also guides how communities of faith interact and support each other.

- **Continual Reflection and Teaching:** Paul's reflection on his experience on the Damascus road continues to influence his theological contributions, leading to teachings that challenge and redefine traditional views of sin, punishment, and redemption within the early Christian communities.

Conclusion

In "No Condemination," the narrative of Paul's encounter with Christ illustrates a shift from expected judgment to an experience of profound grace. This chapter explores how this theme of grace versus condemnation permeates Paul's writings, fundamentally altering Christian theology and personal faith practices. It challenges believers to live in the freedom of grace, rejecting condemnation, and to engage with the gospel in a way that transforms understanding and action.

❧

CHAPTER 8

FEAR OF THE LORD

Bible Verse

"So that at the name of Jesus every knee will bow, of those who are in heaven and on earth and under the earth." - Philippians 2:10 (NASB)

Introduction

This chapter explores the profound concept of the "fear of the Lord" as experienced and expressed by Paul following his transformative encounter with Jesus on the road to Damascus. The chapter delves into how this fear is distinct from earthly fear, acting instead as a divine catalyst for reverence and obedience.

Word of Wisdom

"Saul met the resurrected Jesus and was simultaneously aware of the law, aware of the power of God, and aware of his humanity." - This encapsulates the

29

moment of Saul's encounter, highlighting the depth of the fear of the Lord that touched him. Paul Manwaring

Main Theme

The main theme focuses on the tension between the fear of the Lord and the grace of God—a dynamic that profoundly influenced Paul's theology and ministry, guiding his teachings on holiness, salvation, and inter-relational conduct within the Christian community.

Key Points

• Paul's Damascus road experience instilled in him a deep, reverential fear of the Lord.

• This fear did not result in condemnation but led to a profound recognition of God's mercy and grace.

• Paul's teachings often juxtaposed the fear of the Lord with the assurance of God's welcoming love.

• He advocated for living out one's faith with a balance of reverence and grace.

• Fear of the Lord is portrayed as essential for true holiness and relational harmony within the church.

• Paul used his own transformative encounter as a foundation to teach these concepts to early Christian communities.

Key Themes

- **Integrating Fear and Grace:** The chapter underscores the necessity of integrating the fear of the Lord with the understanding of divine grace. This integration forms a healthy foundation for Christian living, where believers respect God's power and holiness while embracing His merciful and gracious nature.
- **Behavioral Transformation Through Divine Fear:** Paul's experience illustrates how the fear of the Lord is not about dread but about awe and reverence that transforms behavior. This fear is essential for understanding the magnitude of grace given through Jesus Christ and is a catalyst for profound personal and communal transformation.
- **Theological Depth of Fear:** The fear of the Lord offers a theological depth to understanding God's interactions with humanity. It enriches the believers' appreciation of God's nature as both just and merciful, encouraging a fuller, more respectful engagement with His commandments and promises.
- **Practical Applications in Church Teachings:** Paul's letters to the Corinthians, Philippians, and Ephesians highlight the practical applications of living in the fear of the Lord—ranging from pursuing holiness to fostering mutual respect among believers. This fear underpins ethical living and deepens the

believers' commitment to the faith community.

- **Personal and Collective Impact:** The fear of the Lord impacts both individual believers and the collective church. It influences personal sanctification and shapes communal dynamics, serving as a reminder of God's omnipotence and the ultimate accountability to His divine authority.

Conclusion

Chapter Eight of the book elucidates how the fear of the Lord, as experienced by Paul, is crucial for a balanced Christian life that harmonizes reverence with grace. This biblical fear is foundational for personal growth, theological understanding, and communal health within the church. It encourages believers to live in a manner that honors God's holiness while also receiving His grace with humility and gratitude.

❦

CHAPTER 9

RECONCILIATION

Bible Verse
"Brother Saul." - Acts 9:17

Introduction

This chapter delves into the transformative reconciliation that occurred between Saul and Ananias, symbolizing Saul's shift from persecutor to apostle through an encounter filled with divine grace. It emphasizes how personal reconciliation reflects a broader theme of spiritual and communal harmony.

Word of Wisdom

"Trust and obey is the requirement placed upon us; we may never know the eternal fruit, but the internal and eternal rewards are assured." Paul Manwaring

Main Theme

The theme of reconciliation not only captures the personal transformation of Saul but also illustrates the power of forgiveness and acceptance in overcoming historical divisions and animosities.

Key Points

• The Nabi prophet is characterized by a fluent outpouring of words inspired by the Spirit.

• Seer prophets experience God through visions and senses, often resulting in emotionally charged revelations.

• Watchman prophets are vigilant, interceding and warning against spiritual dangers.

• Prophets should not limit themselves to a single mode of revelation but embrace all ways God communicates.

• Each type of prophet has strengths and weaknesses; a balanced ministry requires developing in all areas.

Key Themes

• **Transformation Through Reconciliation:** The encounter between Saul and Ananias is depicted as a pivotal moment of spiritual and personal transformation. It is through this act of reconciliation that Saul fully steps into his new identity in Christ, illustrating the potential for change even in the most unlikely individuals.

- **Role of Divine Guidance in Reconciliation:** Both Saul and Ananias acted under divine guidance, showing that true reconciliation often requires obedience to God's direction, even when it goes against personal or communal biases.
- **Impact of Reconciliation on Broader Missions:** Saul's reconciliation with Ananias was not just a personal victory but a strategic realignment of his life's mission. This act of acceptance empowered him to bridge the divides between Jewish and Gentile believers, enriching the early Christian community.
- **Symbolic and Practical Aspects of Reconciliation:** The simple greeting, "Brother Saul," serves as a powerful symbol of forgiveness and acceptance, which are crucial for genuine reconciliation. This greeting underscores the shift from hostility to fellowship and from judgment to grace.
- **Continuous Ripple Effects of Reconciliation:** The narrative suggests that moments of reconciliation can have lasting impacts, extending beyond the individuals immediately involved. Saul's transformation influenced his teachings and the lives of early Christians, demonstrating the enduring power of reconciliatory actions.

Conclusion

Chapter Nine of the book paints a vivid picture of the critical role that reconciliation plays in spiritual transformation and community building. Through the lens of Saul's encounter with Ananias, we see how acts of forgiveness and acceptance can lead to profound personal changes and contribute to the healing and unity of entire communities. This story serves as a timeless reminder of the power of grace to transcend past animosities and forge new, peaceful relationships.

CHAPTER 10

THE VOICE

Bible Verse
"Now faith is the assurance of things hoped for, the
conviction of things not seen." - Hebrews 11:1
NASB95

Introduction

C hapter Ten explores the profound impact
of hearing God's voice, as exemplified by
Paul's transformative encounter on the
road to Damascus. This chapter discusses the di-
chotomy between the audible voice heard by Paul
and the "still small voice" that many believers experience, emphasizing the life-changing power of divine communication.

Word of Wisdom

"Faith is only known in the unseen."
Paul Manwaring

Main Theme

The central theme focuses on the role of God's voice in guiding and transforming lives, using Paul's experience as a foundational example of how divine intervention redirects and empowers believers.

Key Points

• Paul's encounter with the audible voice of Jesus radically changed his life direction and beliefs.

• His writings frequently reflect the certainty and authority he gained from hearing Jesus' voice.

• Paul's experience underscores the obedience that comes from faith, a key message in his letters.

• The voice of God provides boundaries and direction, serving as a catalyst for personal and spiritual growth.

• Paul's confidence in his mission was bolstered by the clear, divine instructions he received, which set him apart from his companions who heard only thunder.

• The chapter asserts that personal encounters with God's voice are crucial for individual faith journeys.

Key Themes

• **Contrast Between Human Expectation and Divine Intervention:**
Paul's experience on the Damascus road illustrates the stark contrasts between human plans and God's interventions. This

encounter highlights how the voice of God often comes unexpectedly but brings clear direction and purpose, reshaping lives in profound ways.

- **Synergy and Tension in Faith and Obedience:** There is a deep connection and sometimes tension between faith and obedience as shown by Paul's response to hearing God's voice. His transformation emphasizes that true obedience springs from faith rooted in divine revelation, not merely human understanding.

- **Impact of Divine Voice on Personal Mission:** Hearing God's voice not only redirected Paul's life but also defined his apostolic mission, underscoring the transformative power of divine communication. His subsequent writings and actions were deeply influenced by the certainty and authority of that divine encounter.

- **The Role of Faith in Recognizing God's Voice:** The chapter explores the necessity of faith in recognizing and responding to God's voice, as seen in Paul's life. This theme is crucial for believers, as it calls for a reliance on spiritual rather than physical senses to discern God's guidance.

- **Historical and Personal Significance of God's Voice:** Paul's story is used to demonstrate that hearing from God is not just a biblical narrative but a personal journey that continues to resonate with believers today. His experience connects with the broader biblical tradition of divine encounters that guide and define destinies.

Conclusion

Chapter Ten of the book "The Voice" eloquently captures the essence of divine communication as a pivotal element in Christian faith. Through the lens of Paul's transformative encounter with Jesus, the chapter highlights how hearing God's voice can dramatically redirect one's life path and deepen one's faith. It invites readers to seek and value these moments of divine intervention, reinforcing the belief that God's voice remains a powerful force in shaping personal and collective Christian journeys.

KNOWN BY THE SPIRIT

Bible Verse

"Therefore if anyone is in Christ, he is a new creature; the old things passed away; behold, new things have come." - 2 Corinthians 5:17 NASB95

Introduction

Chapter Eleven delves into the transformative recognition Paul experienced through his encounter with Jesus on the road to Damascus, emphasizing how being known by the Spirit reshapes one's identity and future.

Word of Wisdom

"He was identified as a chosen vessel."
Paul Manwaring

Main Theme

This chapter explores the concept of divine recognition and transformation, highlighting how spiritual encounters can redefine our self-perception and align us with God's vision for our lives.

Key Points

• Paul was recognized by Jesus not just as he was, but as he could be—a chosen vessel for spreading the Gospel.

• The encounter marked a complete transformation for Paul, altering his life's mission and self-identity.

• Paul teaches that in Christ, we become entirely new creatures, leaving our pasts behind.

• His teachings emphasize the importance of seeing ourselves as God sees us, fully transformed and redeemed.

• The concept of being a new creature in Christ is likened to a marriage where the past is buried, allowing for a new union with Christ.

• Paul's letters reflect his ongoing struggle and reconciliation with his past and his divine calling.

Key Themes

• **Transformation Through Divine Encounter:** Paul's transformation on the road to Damascus is presented as a profound shift from persecutor to apostle, demonstrating the power of divine encounters to completely change one's direction and identity. This moment is highlighted as a pivot point where Saul's past was redeemed and his future as Paul was unleashed.

- **Spiritual Identity and New Creation:** The chapter emphasizes the spiritual rebirth that occurs when one is "in Christ," using Paul's life as an example of this radical change. It discusses how believers must embrace their new identities and see themselves through the lens of Christ's redemption and grace.

- **The Impact of Divine Recognition on Self-Perception:** Paul's reflection on his past and his new mission illustrates the impact of Christ's recognition on one's self-perception. This transformation encourages believers to view their pasts not as chains but as steps towards their divinely orchestrated futures.

- **Humility and Divine Tension:** The tension between understanding one's unworthiness due to past sins and embracing the greatness of one's divine calling is explored. This tension is necessary for walking in humility and fulfilling one's purpose without falling into pride or self-deprecation.

- **Reconciliation with One's Past:** The narrative of Paul's encounter with Jesus on the Damascus road is used to explore the theme of reconciliation with one's past. It underscores that believers are not defined by their past actions but by their current and future identities in Christ, enabling

them to move forward in hope and
confidence.

Conclusion

Chapter Eleven of the book "Known by the Spirit"
offers a compelling look at the transformative
power of being known by God, through the lens of
Paul's dramatic encounter with Jesus. It challenges
readers to see themselves as God sees them—
forgiven, renewed, and destined for a purpose
greater than their pasts. This chapter encourages
believers to embrace their new identities in Christ,
recognizing that true transformation is both a
spiritual rebirth and a continual process of
becoming who God has called them to be.

☙❧

CHAPTER 12

BLIND EYES

Bible Verse

"To open their eyes so that they may turn from
darkness to light" - Acts 26:18 NASB

Introduction

Chapter Twelve delves into the symbolism
and transformational impact of Saul's temporary physical blindness during his encounter with Jesus, paralleling this with his spiritual
ministry to bring sight to the spiritually blind.

Word of Wisdom

*"He declared Elymas blind and de-
clared that he had come to bring sight to
the blind, and it began with his personal
experience in the dust and dirt of that
road."*

Main Theme

This chapter explores the profound symbolism of blindness in Paul's life and teachings, illustrating how physical blindness mirrored the spiritual blindness he aimed to heal through his ministry.

Key Points

• Saul's physical blindness during his conversion is mirrored later when he renders Elymas blind, emphasizing the theme of spiritual sight and blindness in his ministry.

• This experience profoundly shaped Paul's understanding and ministry, focusing on bringing spiritual sight to those blinded by unbelief.

• Paul's own healing from blindness symbolizes the Messiah's role as a healer, fulfilling prophetic signs through personal experience.

• The theme of spiritual sight and blindness permeates Paul's writings and teachings, reinforcing the transformative power of Christ's light.

• Paul's prayers for believers to receive spiritual sight echo his personal journey from blindness to sight, highlighting his deep empathy and understanding of spiritual enlightenment.

Key Themes

• **Symbolism of Blindness and Sight:** Paul's temporary blindness is not just a personal affliction but a powerful symbol of his previous spiritual state. This theme is recurrent in his ministry, where he uses his experience to empathize with and heal others who are spiritually blind.

- **Transformation Through Divine Intervention:** Paul's blindness and subsequent healing underscore the transformative intervention of Jesus. This personal miracle becomes a cornerstone for his teachings on spiritual enlightenment and the opening of spiritual eyes.

- **Empathy and Authority in Ministry:** Paul's experience with blindness gives him unique authority and empathy in his ministry. He understands the profound impact of receiving one's sight—both physically and spiritually—and this understanding informs his approach to teaching and healing.

- **Spiritual Sight as a Metaphor for Salvation:** The recovery of his sight symbolizes Paul's salvation and call to ministry, serving as a metaphor for the spiritual awakening he wishes to bring to others. This personal transformation highlights the broader theme of turning from darkness to light through Christ.

- **Continuous Revelation and Knowledge of Christ:** Paul emphasizes the importance of continuing to grow in the knowledge of Christ, suggesting that spiritual sight deepens with an ongoing relationship with Jesus. His prayers for believers reflect his desire for them to experience continual spiritual revelations as he did.

Conclusion

Chapter Twelve of "Blind Eyes" illustrates how Paul's physical blindness and subsequent healing profoundly influenced his spiritual insights and ministry. It underscores the themes of transformation, spiritual enlightenment, and the continual need for growth in the knowledge of Christ. Paul uses his own dramatic transformation from blindness to sight as a powerful narrative to encourage believers to seek and cherish their spiritual vision, emphasizing the transformative power of encountering Christ.

❧

CHAPTER 13

THE LETTERS

Bible Verse

"Our adequacy is from God, who also made us adequate as servants of a new covenant, not of the letter but of the spirit; for the letter kills, but the Spirit gives life." - 2 Corinthians 3:5-6 NASB

Introduction

This chapter explores the transformational journey of Saul from carrying letters of death to writing letters of life, emphasizing how his physical letters to the high priest contrast with the spiritual letters he would later write as Paul.

Word of Wisdom

"Sometimes we need letters of commendation, and other times we need to

trust the commendation we have already received." Paul Manwaring

Main Theme

The chapter delves into the metaphorical and literal significance of letters in Paul's life, illustrating how his initial mission under the authority of the high priest transformed into a spiritual mission under the Great High Priest, Jesus Christ.

Key Points

• Saul initially carried letters authorizing him to persecute Christians, representing his old life and mission.

• His encounter on the road to Damascus transformed him from a bearer of death to a writer of life.

• Paul used the metaphor of being a letter from Christ to the Corinthians, emphasizing the personal transformation each believer undergoes.

• He argued that the letter of the law kills, but the Spirit gives life, contrasting his old and new missions.

• Paul's writings themselves became letters inscribed not on paper, but on the hearts of believers, carrying divine authority and eternal significance.

Key Themes

- **Transformation from Death to Life:** Paul's transformation from carrying letters that brought death to writing ones that offer spiritual life highlights the profound change in his mission post-encounter. His role shifted from enforcing the law to spreading the gospel, symbolizing the transition from the letter of the law to the spirit of grace.

- **Spiritual vs. Literal Letters:** The concept of letters transitions from a literal to a spiritual metaphor in Paul's teachings. He discusses how the letters he once carried, which were meant to bring death, were replaced by spiritual letters written on the hearts of believers, emphasizing the life-giving power of the Holy Spirit over the condemning power of the law.

- **Personal and Corporate Transformation:** Paul's letters to various churches illustrate not only his personal transformation but also his vision for the transformation of the entire Christian community. Through his epistles, he nurtures, guides, and shapes the early Christian faith across different cultures and geographies.

- **The Enduring Power of Written Word:** Paul's epistles have transcended time and culture, becoming foundational texts that continue to instruct and inspire millions. This legacy highlights the enduring power of the written word when guided by divine inspiration.

- **Letters as Tools of Commendation and Authority:** Paul discusses the concept of letters of commendation, both those he carried and those he wrote, as tools of authority and authenticity in his ministry. He challenges believers to recognize the divine commendation they receive through their faith and transformation in Christ.

Conclusion

Chapter Thirteen of "The Letters" reflects on the pivotal role that letters played in Paul's life, from the physical letters he carried on the road to Damascus to the spiritual letters he wrote as an apostle. Through this narrative, the chapter illuminates the transformational power of divine encounters and the shift from adhering to the letter of the law to embracing the life-giving spirit of the new covenant. This journey from death to life encapsulates the essence of Paul's ministry and his message to all believers.

CHAPTER 14

THE RESURRECTED JESUS

Bible Verse

"For as often as you eat this bread and drink the cup, you proclaim the Lord's death until He comes." - 1 Corinthians 11:26 NASB

Introduction

This chapter delves into Paul's transformation following his direct encounter with the resurrected Jesus on the road to Damascus, exploring how this singular event reframed his entire theological outlook and ministry, making the resurrection central to his preaching and writings.

Word of Wisdom

"Paul was led to Jesus by Jesus, and Jesus would later teach him even about the communion service." Paul Manwaring

Main Theme

The chapter explores the profound impact of encountering the resurrected Jesus directly, how this experience became the cornerstone of Paul's theology, and its continuous influence in his ministry and writings, especially concerning the Eucharist.

Key Points

• Paul's only direct encounter with Jesus was with the resurrected form, setting the foundation for his entire ministry.

• This encounter led Paul to focus intensely on the resurrection as the core of the Christian faith.

• Paul's insights into communion and the Last Supper teachings were divinely revealed, though he was not physically present at the event.

• His writings frequently return to the theme of resurrection, emphasizing its necessity for Christian faith and preaching.

• The transformation from persecutor to apostle highlights the radical change possible through divine encounter.

Key Themes

• Jesus led to an obsession with the resurrected Christ, influencing every aspect of his ministry. This obsession is mirrored in Paul's deep theological reflections and the central theme of resurrection in his writings, demonstrating how profound encounters can shape one's focus and mission.

- **Divine Revelation of Communion:** Paul's detailed account of the Last Supper, despite not being present, indicates a direct revelation from Jesus. This teaching underscores the importance of communion in Christian practice and its theological implications about Jesus' sacrifice and promise of return.

- **Transformation through Encounter:** The chapter highlights how direct encounters with the divine can drastically transform beliefs and behaviors. Paul's transformation from a persecutor of Christians to a principal figure in Christianity exemplifies the radical change that divine intervention can effectuate.

- **Resurrection as Central Doctrine:** The resurrection of Jesus is central to Paul's preaching and is emphasized as the cornerstone of Christian hope and faith. His arguments against those who deny the resurrection underscore its importance for the validity of Christian doctrine and personal faith.

- **Continual Divine Instruction:** Paul's ongoing encounters with Jesus after Damascus provided him with insights that he would share through his letters. These encounters underline the concept that initial conversion is just the beginning of a lifelong journey of divine instruction and deepening understanding.

Conclusion

Chapter Fourteen, "The Resurrected Jesus," reveals how the resurrection was not only central to Paul's conversion but remained a pivotal theme throughout his ministry. By focusing on how Paul's initial and ongoing encounters with Jesus shaped his theological directives and pastoral practices, the chapter illustrates the transformative power of encountering the divine, especially the resurrected Christ, who turns persecutors into prophets and enemies into evangelists.

CHAPTER 15

THE SPIRIT OF ADOPTION

Bible Verse

"But you have received a spirit of adoption as sons by which we cry out, 'Abba! Father!'" - Romans 8:15 NASB95

Introduction

This chapter explores the profound concept of spiritual adoption as understood and articulated by Paul following his transformative encounter on the road to Damascus. It delves into how this encounter may have shaped his understanding of being spiritually adopted by God, highlighting the depth of relational and identity change that comes with it.

Word of Wisdom

"We have already received the spirit of adoption—we received it at conversion."
Paul Manwaring

Main Theme

The chapter discusses the theme of spiritual adoption in Christianity, emphasizing how this divine relationship reshapes our identity, privileges, and responsibilities as believers. It connects Paul's dramatic conversion and subsequent teachings to the broader Christian experience of being adopted into God's family.

Key Points

• Paul's Damascus road encounter likely initiated his deep understanding of spiritual adoption.

• Spiritual adoption is presented as a transformation from being outside to fully belonging within God's family.

• This theme is woven throughout Paul's letters, particularly in Romans, where he explicates our new identity as God's children.

• Paul teaches that this adoption occurs at conversion, involving a profound recognition of our new status before God.

• The concept is tied to a complete transformation, akin to moving from slavery to sonship.

Key Themes

- **Immediate and Complete Transformation:** Paul's encounter not only converted him from persecutor to preacher but also shifted his spiritual status from outsider to adopted son. This immediate transformation is a hallmark of his teachings, emphasizing that spiritual adoption is both instantaneous and comprehensive, reshaping our identity and relationships fundamentally.

- **Relational Depth of Adoption:** Spiritual adoption, as described by Paul, transcends legal or formal changes; it is deeply relational. This adoption brings us into an intimate relationship with God, allowing us to address Him as 'Abba, Father' and reassures us of our full acceptance and loved status within His family.

- **Legacy of Sonship and Inheritance:** By focusing on adoption, Paul underscores our legacy as co-heirs with Christ, entitling us to share in both the sufferings and the glory of Jesus. This dual participation underlines the serious and glorious implications of our new identity.

- **Practical Outworking of Adoption:** The spirit of adoption compels believers to live in recognition of their new reality, influencing their behavior, interactions, and self-perception. Paul's own life exemplifies this, as he consistently lived out the implications of his sonship, which included suffering for the sake of the Gospel.

- **Universal Invitation to Adoption:** Paul's teachings extend the invitation of adoption to all believers, emphasizing that this profound change is available to everyone who comes to faith in Christ.

This inclusivity is pivotal to understanding the broad and transformative impact of the Gospel.

Conclusion

Chapter Fifteen, "The Spirit of Adoption," beautifully encapsulates the transformative and relational essence of becoming a child of God through faith in Christ. By weaving together Paul's personal experience and theological insights, the chapter invites readers to deeply consider the implications of being adopted by God, not just as a theological concept but as a living, breathing reality that changes every aspect of a believer's life and identity.

CHAPTER 16

BOUGHT WITH A PRICE

Bible Verse

"For you have been bought with a price." - 1
Corinthians 6:20 NASB

Introduction

T his chapter delves into Paul's profound realization of being "bought with a price," a concept that profoundly influenced his teachings and reflections on grace, sacrifice, and redemption. It explores how his encounter with Jesus on the Damascus road crystallized his understanding of the immense cost of his spiritual freedom.

Word of Wisdom

"It is no longer I who live, but Christ lives in me." - Galatians 2:20 NASB

Main Theme

The chapter emphasizes the transformative realization Paul experienced regarding the price paid for his redemption, reflecting on how this understanding shaped his theology and ministry.

Key Points

• Paul's encounter with Jesus revealed his high value in the eyes of God.

• He recognized the price of his redemption intertwined with the teachings of Jesus and the prophecies of the Old Testament.

• His writings often reflect on the concept of being purchased by Christ's sacrifice.

• Paul connects the notion of being bought with a price to living a life that reflects Christ's life within us.

• The idea of redemption and sacrifice is central to Paul's message to the early churches.

Key Themes

- **Understanding the Price of Redemption:** Paul's Damascus road encounter instilled a deep awareness of the cost of his salvation. This realization that he was a "vessel of mercy" chosen by God underscores much of his later teachings, emphasizing the sacrificial love and patience of Christ.
- **Grace Coupled with Responsibility:** While Paul deeply appreciated the grace

he received, he also understood the weight of the responsibility it entailed. His teachings encourage believers to live in a manner worthy of the sacrifice made for them, highlighting a life transformed by gratitude and purpose.

- **Theological Depth of Redemption:** Paul's reflections on being bought at a price explore the theological depths of justification, resurrection, and righteousness. He eloquently connects these doctrines to offer a comprehensive understanding of Christian salvation as seen through the lens of his own conversion.

- **Personal Transformation Through Redemption:** The theme of redemption is not just theological but intensely personal for Paul. It changed his identity from a persecutor of Christians to a proponent of the faith, highlighting the personal transformation that accompanies the acceptance of Christ's sacrifice.

- **Legacy of Redemption:** Paul's awareness of being bought with a price is a legacy he passes on through his letters, instilling in his readers a sense of value and purpose that transcends their past sins and failures. He uses his own life as a testament to the transformative power of accepting Jesus's lordship and sacrifice.

Conclusion

Chapter Sixteen, "Bought with a Price," captures the essence of Paul's transformation from a persecutor of Christians to a pillar of the Church, driven by his encounter with the resurrected Jesus. It beautifully articulates how the realization of being bought with a price—Christ's own life—reshaped Paul's identity and mission, encouraging believers to live lives that reflect the profound sacrifice made for their redemption.

CHAPTER 17

SAUL'S COMPANIONS

Bible Verse

"For if you were to have countless tutors in Christ, yet you would not have many fathers, for in Christ Jesus I became your father through the gospel. Therefore I exhort you, be imitators of me." - 1 Corinthians 4:15-16 NASB

Introduction

This chapter explores the significant impact of Saul's companions on his journey to Damascus and how his transformative encounter with Jesus influenced his relationships and teachings about spiritual fatherhood and companionship.

Word of Wisdom

"Countless tutors without fathers is inadequate. Teachers give knowledge, but it

needs the father's example." Paul Manwaring

Main Theme

The chapter discusses the role of companionship in spiritual transformation and leadership, emphasizing how personal encounters with Jesus shape our relational dynamics and leadership styles.

Key Points

• Saul's companions on the road to Damascus played a crucial role in the immediate aftermath of his conversion.

• These companions witnessed Saul's transformation firsthand, influencing their future paths.

• Paul emphasizes the value of spiritual fatherhood over mere instruction in his later writings.

• The shift from teacher to father figure is a central theme in Paul's approach to leadership and mentorship.

• Paul's experience with his companions illustrates the importance of accountable, transformative relationships in Christian ministry.

Key Themes

• **Transformative Relationships:** Saul's journey with his unnamed companions highlights the profound impact of shared spiritual experiences on relationships. His transformation led to a redefinition of his relational dynamics, emphasizing the importance of being surrounded by those who are committed to the same spiritual path.

- **Spiritual Fatherhood:** Paul's writings often reflect on the need for spiritual fathers, not just teachers, within the Christian community. This concept was likely influenced by his own transformation and the paternal role he assumed in the lives of those he led to Christ, demonstrating the depth and commitment required in spiritual mentorship.

- **The Role of Companions in Ministry:** The companions who traveled with Saul were integral to his initial transformation and continued to play a role in his ministry. Their willingness to follow Saul into new spiritual territories underscores the necessity of supportive companions in ministry.

- **Accountability and Example in Leadership:** Paul's transition from Saul emphasizes accountability and the example set by leaders. His life became a model for others not just in words but in actions, showing that true leadership in the Christian context is about living out the teachings of Christ visibly and authentically.

- **The Impact of Personal Encounter:** Saul's encounter on the road didn't just change him; it also set a precedent for those around him. It shows how personal transformation can have wide-reaching effects on one's community and beyond, particularly when that transformation is shared openly and integrated into one's life and mission.

Conclusion

Chapter Seventeen, "Saul's Companions," delves into the crucial role of companionship in spiritual transformation and leadership. By examining the dynamics between Saul and his companions, the chapter illustrates how transformative experiences with Christ can redefine relationships and leadership styles, emphasizing the need for spiritual fatherhood and accountable relationships within the Christian community.

৩৯৩

CHAPTER 18

THE UNAPPROACHABLE
LIGHT

Bible Verse

"Who alone possesses immortality and dwells in
unapproachable light, whom no man has seen or
can see." - 1 Timothy 6:16 NASB

Introduction

This chapter explores the profound
revelation Paul experienced of God's "unapproachable light," inspired by his Damascus road encounter, linking it to a deeper
understanding of divine holiness and the spiritual
implications of light in scripture.

Word of Wisdom

*"In a world of scientific developments,
we can forget the raw power of the sun.
It cleanses, bleaches, sanitizes, and exposes." Paul Manwaring*

Main Theme

Paul's encounter with the divine light not only transformed his physical sight but also his spiritual perception, deepening his theological insights into the nature of God's holiness and purity.

Key Points

• Paul encountered a light brighter than the sun on the road to Damascus, leading to his temporary blindness.

• This experience paralleled that of Moses, who also encountered God's glory and had to wear a veil.

• Paul used this concept of divine light to instruct Timothy on living a holy life.

• The unapproachable light is a metaphor for God's absolute purity and separation from sin.

• Paul integrates this theme of light throughout his teachings, emphasizing its role in exposing and cleansing sin.

Key Themes

• **Divine Encounter and Transformation:** Paul's encounter with the heavenly light was a pivotal moment that profoundly shaped his theology. This light, symbolizing God's pure holiness, led Paul to a deeper understanding of God's nature, which he articulated through his letters, teaching believers about the significance of living in reverence and godliness.

- **Historical and Theological Parallels:** Comparing his experience to that of Moses, Paul draws a direct line between the key figures of the faith and their encounters with God's glory. This historical parallel serves to validate his apostolic authority and deepens the understanding of divine encounters across scripture.

- **Spiritual Illumination and Exposure:** Paul emphasizes that just as natural light exposes and cleanses, so does the spiritual light of God. This theme is crucial in understanding how believers are to live in transparency, purity, and truth under God's holy scrutiny.

- **Instruction and Exhortation:** The experience of the unapproachable light not only informs Paul's personal faith but also his pastoral instructions. He uses this concept to exhort Timothy and others to pursue righteousness and maintain purity in anticipation of Christ's return.

- **Continuous Revelation and Impact:** Paul's reflections on the unapproachable light illustrate his ongoing theological reflection and revelation post-conversion. His teachings aim to elevate believers' views of God's majesty and the serious call to holiness that stems from understanding God's true nature.

Conclusion

Chapter Eighteen, "The Unapproachable Light,"
delves into the transformative impact of Paul's
encounter with the divine light on his theology and
ministry. By analyzing his reflections and teachings
on this theme, the chapter highlights the profound
spiritual truths about God's purity and holiness
that Paul experienced firsthand and passionately
imparted to early Christians, urging them to live
lives worthy of the high calling in Christ.

CHAPTER 19

UNINVITED AND UNWANTED

Bible Verse
"Not that we loved God, but that He loved us." - 1
John 4:10 NASB

Introduction

This chapter reflects on the unexpected and unwanted nature of Saul's conversion on the road to Damascus, illustrating the profound concept that God actively pursues even those who are not seeking Him, reshaping our understanding of divine predestination and free will.

Word of Wisdom

"Allow me the luxury of living in the mystery of saying that I prefer to embrace the tension." Paul Manwaring

Main Theme

The chapter explores the sovereignty of God's intervention in Saul's life, highlighting the theme of divine pursuit despite human resistance or indifference, and the transformation that follows an encounter with God.

Key Points

• Saul's encounter with Jesus was neither sought after nor expected, showcasing God's initiative in the act of salvation.

• The concept of predestination is explored through the lens of Saul's transformative encounter.

• God's pursuit is seen as an act of grace that is often unexpected and always undeserved.

• The narrative challenges the notion that individuals find God through their own efforts.

• Saul's life post-encounter becomes a testimony to the relentless and transforming love of God.

• The chapter emphasizes the coexistence of God's sovereignty with human free will in the mystery of salvation.

Key Themes

• **Divine Sovereignty and Human Response:** The chapter examines the tension between God's sovereign will and human free will, using Saul's conversion as a primary example. It discusses how God's initiating love and pursuit of individuals does not negate the human response but rather invites it.

- **Transformation through Divine Encounter:** Saul's conversion is portrayed as a pivotal example of how divine encounters can lead to profound personal transformation and reorientation of life's goals and actions. This transformation is not just spiritual but encompasses the totality of one's being and purpose.

- **The Role of Grace in Salvation:** The unwanted nature of Saul's encounter underscores the role of grace in salvation— emphasizing that God's choice to save is rooted in His own goodness and mercy rather than human merit or desire.

- **Predestination and Calling:** The chapter delves into the theological implications of predestination, suggesting that Paul's reflection on his own experience provides a unique insight into how God calls and equips those He has chosen for specific purposes.

- **Reflection and Application for Believers:** Readers are encouraged to reflect on their own experiences of being pursued by God, recognizing that divine encounters are not always sought but often come in moments of unexpected grace, transforming lives in ways that align with God's sovereign purposes.

Conclusion

"Uninvited and Unwanted" offers a deep exploration of the involuntary aspects of divine encounters, illustrating through Saul's dramatic conversion how God's pursuit of individuals transcends human willingness or readiness. The chapter encourages readers to embrace the mystery of God's sovereignty and grace, acknowledging that the most transformative encounters with God often come when least expected, leading to a life wholly dedicated to His purposes.

CHAPTER 20

RELATIONAL

Bible Verse

"And you will know the truth, and the truth will
set you free." - John 8:31 NASB

Introduction

This chapter explores the transformation of
Saul's journey from a mission of persecution to one of profound relational connection with Jesus, marking the beginning of his
transformation into Paul. The chapter emphasizes
the shift from transactional to relational dynamics
in Saul's life and subsequent ministry.

Word of Wisdom

"Truth, of course, is a person." Paul
Manwaring

Main Theme

The central theme is the transition from Saul's rigid and transactional understanding of faith to a deeply relational, transformative encounter with Jesus, reshaping his entire approach to ministry and theology.

Key Points

• Saul's original mission was punitive and harsh, aimed at quelling the spread of Christianity.

• His encounter with Jesus on the Damascus road was a pivotal relational introduction that changed his life's trajectory.

• This encounter shifted Saul's focus from persecution to preaching and relational ministry.

• Saul's theology was deeply influenced by this transformative meeting, emphasizing relational knowledge over academic.

• The theme of relational engagement is central in Paul's later writings and ministry.

• The relational aspect of Saul's conversion illustrates a divine approach that personalizes and humanizes theological understanding.

Key Themes

• **Transformation through Relational Encounters:** Saul's encounter with Jesus illustrates a dramatic shift from a life of religious rigidity to one of relational engagement. This moment of transformation underscores the importance of personal encounters with Jesus in understanding and living out the Christian faith.

- **The Impact of Divine Introduction:** The way Jesus introduced Himself to Saul highlights the personal nature of divine encounters. Instead of condemnation, Jesus offered a relationship, which fundamentally altered Saul's identity and purpose.
- **Relational Theology:** Saul's subsequent teachings as Paul emphasize the importance of relationships both with Christ and within the community of believers. His letters advocate for a shift from a law-based faith to one that is founded on the relational grace through Jesus Christ.
- **From Knowledge to Relationship:** Paul's writings often reflect his journey from a knowledge-based practice of religion to a relationship-oriented walk with God. This shift is evident in his emphasis on knowing Christ personally and intimately as opposed to merely understanding theological concepts.
- **Ministry of Reconciliation:** Drawing from his personal transformation, Paul emphasizes the ministry of reconciliation, urging believers to embody the relational nature of the gospel in their dealings with others. This ministry is not just about spreading the gospel but about fostering

deep, genuine relationships that reflect Christ's love and unity.

Conclusion

Chapter Twenty delves into the relational essence of Paul's transformation from Saul, the persecutor, to a leading apostle who deeply understood and communicated the essence of relational Christianity. His encounter with Jesus not only changed his theological approach but also his understanding of divine and human relationships, emphasizing that the core of Christianity is relational, not transactional.

❧

CHAPTER 21

POWER

Bible Verse

"But we have this treasure in jars of clay to show that this all-surpassing power is from God and not from us." - 2 Corinthians 4:7 (NIV)

Introduction

Chapter Twenty-One recounts Saul's transformative encounter with divine power on his journey to Damascus. Initially intent on persecuting followers of the Way with his human authority and strength, Saul is instead overwhelmed by God's immense power, leading to a profound personal and ministerial transformation.

Word of Wisdom

"He doesn't come with clever words, but with a demonstration of power." Paul Manwaring

Main Theme

The chapter explores the theme of divine intervention and the transformative power of God, focusing on how Saul's encounter reshaped his life and ministry from one of persecution to one of profound spiritual leadership.

Key Points

• Saul's journey to Damascus was initially fueled by his own authority and intent to persecute Christians.

• A divine encounter on the road drastically altered Saul's life and purpose.

• Saul's experience symbolizes the exchange of human power for divine authority.

• Following his conversion, Saul, now Paul, emphasized the role of divine power through his teachings and writings.

• Paul often spoke of power, using the term extensively in his epistles to convey the essence of a faith driven by divine strength.

• His ministry was characterized by signs, wonders, and miracles as evidence of true apostolic authority.

Key Themes

- **Divine Confrontation and Transformation:** Saul's confrontation with divine power not only halted his persecution of Christians but also led to his own spiritual rebirth. This pivotal moment is a testament to how divine encounters can redirect life's path and redefine one's purpose.

- **Authentic Apostleship:** Paul's transformation authenticates the characteristics of true apostleship, which he defines as marked by perseverance and accompanied by signs, wonders, and miracles, underscoring that genuine ministry is powered by God, not human strength.

- **Continuity of Divine Power in Ministry:** Throughout his ministry, Paul continuously experienced and demonstrated the power of God. This unending experience shaped his message and his missionary work, emphasizing the necessity of divine power in the life of believers.

- **The Impact of Divine Power on Teaching:** Paul's teachings often focused on the concept of power, which he discussed extensively in his letters to the early churches, particularly highlighting that the gospel comes not only in words but in power.

- **Legacy of Power:** Paul's legacy teaches that the Christian faith is not a mere acceptance of doctrine but a dynamic encounter with God's power, which should be evident in the lives of believers through their actions and spiritual gifts.

Conclusion

Chapter Twenty-One vividly illustrates how a direct encounter with God's power can profoundly transform an individual from persecutor to proponent. Paul's life and teachings serve as a compelling testimony to the enduring truth that genuine faith manifests through divine power, challenging believers to seek a deeper, more authentic experience with God.

CHAPTER 22

RULE KEEPER TO GOD PLEASER

Bible Verse

"But may it never be that I would boast, except in the cross of our Lord Jesus Christ." - Galatians 6:14 NASB

Introduction

This chapter traces Saul's transformation from a stringent Pharisee who sought to please God through strict adherence to religious laws, to becoming Paul, a devoted follower of Christ who sought to please God through a relationship with His Son. It highlights the shift from religion to relationship as the true path to divine connection.

Word of Wisdom

"Religion is form without power." Paul Manwaring

Main Theme

The main theme of this chapter is the transformative power of encountering Jesus Christ, shifting from a life focused on religious formality to one of genuine spiritual relationship.

Key Points

• Saul was a Pharisee deeply involved in religious practices, believing he was serving God by persecuting Christians.

• His dramatic encounter with Jesus on the road to Damascus radically changed his perspective and purpose.

• Paul's ministry shifted from enforcing religious laws to preaching about the power of a personal relationship with Jesus.

• He criticized the empty formality of religion and emphasized the necessity of divine power in genuine godliness.

• Through his writings, Paul conveyed that true godliness involves boasting only in Christ, not in human achievements or adherence to law.

• The legacy of the Pharisees and Sadducees faded, while Christianity, rooted in relationship rather than religion, continues to thrive.

Key Themes

• **Transformation Through Divine Encounter:** Saul's encounter with Jesus was not just a change of heart but a complete transformation of identity from a legalistic Pharisee to a passionate apostle. This shift illustrates the profound impact that a true encounter with God can have on an individual's life and mission.

- **Critique of Religious Formality:** Paul's teachings often focused on the pitfalls of adhering to religious form without understanding its power, highlighting that true faith is not about external compliance but internal transformation and empowerment through Christ.
- **Relationship Over Religion:** The chapter emphasizes that Christianity offers a relationship with God through Jesus Christ, contrasting the temporary and powerless nature of religious forms with the eternal and dynamic nature of spiritual relationship.
- **Enduring Impact of Spiritual Authenticity:** The survival and growth of Christianity, as opposed to the decline of the Pharisees and Sadducees, underscore the lasting influence of a faith that centers on personal relationship rather than mere tradition or formality.
- **Boasting in Christ Alone:** Paul's life post-conversion exemplifies a shift from self-righteousness to Christ-centered righteousness, advocating that true believers boast only in what Jesus has accomplished through the cross, which is the true measure of godliness.

Conclusion

Chapter Twenty-Two encapsulates Saul's transformative journey from a rule-keeping Pharisee to a God-pleasing follower of Christ. His life exemplifies the inadequacy of religious efforts to reach God and the sufficiency of God's grace through Jesus Christ. Paul's transformation and teachings continue to remind us that the essence of true Christianity is not found in rituals or rules, but in a living, dynamic relationship with God.

❀

THE "BUT GOD" FACTOR

Bible Verse

"And not only this, but we also celebrate in our tribulations, knowing that tribulation brings about perseverance; and perseverance, proven character; and proven character, hope; and hope does not disappoint, because the love of God has been poured out within our hearts through the Holy Spirit who was given to us." - Romans 5:3-5 (NASB)

Introduction

This chapter examines the critical moment of transformation for Saul on the road to Damascus, where a divine encounter shifted his life from a religious enforcer to a herald of God's power and grace. The "But God" factor represents the pivotal interventions of God that defy human expectations and reasoning.

Word of Wisdom

"He cannot take you to the wrong appointment." Paul Manwaring

Main Theme

The central theme is the transformative power of divine intervention, specifically how "But God" moments redefine our path, beliefs, and ministry, highlighting Paul's dramatic shift from strict Pharisaism to a life rich with divine experiences and teachings.

Key Points

- Saul's life-altering encounter on the road to Damascus was a "But God" moment that shifted his focus from religion to a relationship with God.
- This encounter became the cornerstone of Paul's message and ministry, emphasizing reliance on divine power rather than human effort.
- Paul's writings frequently reflect on this moment, showcasing its profound impact on his theological understanding.
- His teachings encourage believers to recognize and cherish their own "But God" moments as transformative spiritual experiences.
- Paul's journey underscores the contrast

between empty religious formality and the dynamic power of a lived faith.
- The chapter invites readers to revisit and value their personal encounters with God, recognizing these as foundational to their faith journey.

Key Themes

- **Transformation Through Divine Power:** Paul's transformation illustrates how divine interventions can abruptly shift one's life direction and purpose, moving from self-reliant religiosity to a dependence on God's power and guidance.
- **Foundational Moments of Faith:** The Damascus road encounter did not just change Paul's immediate actions but deeply influenced his entire theological framework, inspiring many of his epistles and teachings about God's overwhelming grace and sovereignty.
- **Embracing the Unexplainable:** The chapter suggests that attempting to fully rationalize divine encounters diminishes their impact; instead, embracing them without full understanding can lead to deeper faith and reliance on God.
- **Impact of "But God" Moments:** These moments are transformative, not only for the individuals directly experiencing them but also for the wider community of believers as they illustrate the power and presence of God in personal and communal trials.

- **Perseverance and Hope:** Drawing from his own experiences, Paul links trials and tribulations to spiritual growth and character development, culminating in a hope that is anchored in God's promises and not circumstantial evidence.

Conclusion

Chapter Twenty-Three eloquently captures the essence of Paul's transformation and the broader concept of "But God" moments that punctuate and redefine the Christian faith journey. It encourages readers to recognize and rely on the divine hand in their lives, assuring them that God's interventions are marked by hope, guidance, and an everlasting impact.

CHAPTER 24

INFORMATIVE AND PROPHETIC

Bible Verse

"In the Lord all the offspring of Israel will be justified and will glory." - Isaiah 45:25 (NASB95)

Introduction

This chapter delves into the dual nature of divine encounters as both informative and prophetic, using the transformative experiences of Saul and Ananias as prime examples. It highlights how detailed instructions from God during these moments are meant to prepare individuals for their future roles and challenges.

Word of Wisdom

"What can I do, and what must I leave to God to do." Paul Manwaring

Main Theme

The main theme focuses on the interplay between receiving direct, practical instructions from God and the broader, prophetic implications of these divine communications that shape the future ministry and personal growth.

Key Points

- Saul and Ananias experienced simultaneous, coordinated divine encounters that were crucial for Saul's transformation and subsequent ministry.
- Saul received specific instructions about his immediate actions and his future mission.
- These divine instructions often come in forms that require both immediate action and long-term contemplation and preparation.
- The prophetic aspect of Saul's encounter outlined not only his future ministry but also the personal sacrifices it would entail.
- Paul's later ministry and writings often reflected back on these prophetic encounters, using them as a foundation for his theological teachings.
- The balance between action and trust in God's timing is a central lesson from these encounters.

Key Themes

- **Detailed Divine Instructions:** Saul's encounter on the road to Damascus serves as a vivid example of how specific and practical God's guidance can be. This guidance not only directed his immediate steps but also set the stage for his lifelong mission.

- **Prophetic Foundations for Ministry:** The prophetic declarations given to Saul about his future challenges and his role in spreading the gospel underscore the depth and foresight of divine encounters. These prophecies shaped Paul's understanding of his mission and his perseverance through trials.

- **Balancing Action with Divine Timing:** Paul's response to his encounter with Jesus illustrates the importance of actively engaging with God's call while also respecting the timing and sequence God has in mind, as shown in his deliberate preparations before fully launching his ministry.

- **The Role of Tribulation in Divine Calling:** Paul's teachings about rejoicing in tribulations and finding hope in them were deeply influenced by the prophecies received during his conversion. His experiences highlight how tribulations are integral to fulfilling God's purpose and developing character.

- **Confirmation and Fulfillment of Prophecy:** Paul's life and ministry not only fulfilled the prophecies about his own life but also served as a confirmation of Old Testament prophecies, demonstrating the continuity and reliability of God's word across the ages.

Conclusion

Chapter Twenty-Four encapsulates how divine encounters are intricately designed to communicate both immediate and future directives from God. These encounters are both practical and prophetic, providing clear instructions for immediate action and illuminating the path for long-term spiritual journeys. Paul's experience exemplifies how adhering to these divine instructions underpins a fruitful ministry and personal transformation.

CHAPTER 25

EMOTIONAL

Bible Verse

"That I may know Him and the power of His resurrection and the fellowship of His sufferings, being conformed to His death." - Philippians 3:10 (NASB)

Introduction

This chapter explores the emotional dimensions of divine encounters, focusing on the intense and life-altering experiences of Paul on the road to Damascus. It underscores the deep emotional impact such encounters can have, shaping one's spiritual journey and ministry.

Word of Wisdom

"We must be prepared to allow our encounters to release our emotions, and to see that it may be the emotions of heav-

*en's family that have initiated the en-
counter in the first place." Paul
Manwaring*

Main Theme

The emotional aspect of divine encounters is pivotal in understanding the profound changes they
can incite in individuals, as vividly illustrated by
Paul's transformative experience and his subsequent teachings that deeply integrate emotional
experiences with spiritual insights.

Key Points

- Paul's conversion was not just a physical or
  spiritual transformation but also an
  intensely emotional experience.
- The emotional response to divine
  encounters can serve to capture our
  attention and direct our focus to God's
  purposes.
- Paul's emotions during his conversion
  linked deeply with the feelings of Jesus,
  highlighting a divine sympathy and
  intentionality.
- His teachings often reflected the
  emotional depth of his experiences,
  guiding others to embrace their own
  spiritual emotions.
- Paul emphasized the importance of
  emotions in experiencing and expressing
  the Christian faith, particularly joy and
  suffering.

Key Themes

- **Integration of Emotion and Spirituality:** The chapter illustrates how emotional responses are integral to spiritual experiences, as seen in Paul's encounter with Jesus. These emotions are not just reactions but are essential components of the encounter, meant to deepen understanding and commitment.

- **Divine Purpose in Emotional Responses:** Emotional reactions to divine encounters are often designed to draw individuals closer to God's heart, helping them to grasp the depth of His plans for them. Paul's emotional journey post-conversion shows how these experiences can lead to profound personal and theological insights.

- **Impact of Emotions on Ministry:** Paul's ministry was heavily influenced by the emotions he experienced during his conversion. His later writings encapsulate this, urging believers to connect deeply with their feelings as they live out their faith.

- **Restorative Justice and Emotional Reconciliation:** The concept of restorative justice, as seen through Paul's teachings and personal experiences, highlights the role of emotions in forgiveness and reconciliation, which are central to the gospel message.

- **Emotions as a Gateway to Spiritual Depth:** By embracing the emotional aspects of their encounters with God, believers can access deeper spiritual truths and experience a fuller relationship with God. Paul's instructions to focus on what is pure, lovely, and praiseworthy encourages believers to cultivate a positive emotional and mental environment.

Conclusion

Chapter Twenty-Five delves into the emotional layers of spiritual encounters, particularly through the lens of Paul's transformation. It shows how emotions are not merely byproducts of divine interactions but are crucial for understanding and engaging with God's purpose. The chapter invites readers to embrace their emotional experiences as vital elements of their spiritual journey, helping them to connect more authentically with God and His kingdom.

UNEXPECTED AND SUDDENLY

Bible Verse

"But seek first the kingdom of God and His righteousness, and all these things shall be added to you." - Matthew 6:33 (NKJV)

Introduction

This chapter discusses the dynamic and dramatic nature of divine interventions, using Paul's sudden conversion as a primary example. It highlights how unexpected, sudden encounters with God can fundamentally transform lives and establish a foundation for future faith and ministry.

Word of Wisdom

"God sometimes takes a long time to act suddenly." Paul Manwaring

Main Theme

The theme focuses on the concept of 'suddenly' moments in the spiritual life, where God intervenes in dramatic and life-changing ways, emphasizing the mixture of immediate transformation and the ongoing process that follows.

Key Points

- Saul's conversion was a sudden, dramatic pivot from persecution to proclamation, illustrating the power of divine 'suddenly' moments.
- These moments are both transformational and foundational, setting the stage for all future spiritual developments and challenges.
- Paul's sudden change instilled in him a belief in the possibility of dramatic divine interventions.
- This belief shaped his ministry and teachings, emphasizing the coexistence of sudden divine actions and ongoing processes.
- Paul's experience underscores the balance between actively waiting for God's timing and being prepared for His sudden moves.

Key Themes

- **The Dramatic Nature of Divine Encounters:** Paul's sudden conversion highlights how divine encounters can occur unexpectedly and dramatically, challenging our perceptions and transforming our life direction instantly.

- **Foundation for Faith:** These sudden moments become foundational for future faith experiences, providing a strong base of testimony that fuels belief in God's ongoing work in our lives and the lives of others.
- **Cultural Shifts in Spiritual Understanding:** Paul's conversion created a culture of expectancy for sudden, divine interventions within the early Christian community, influencing how believers perceive God's actions in their lives.
- **Balancing Patience and Expectancy:** The chapter elaborates on the need to balance the anticipation of sudden divine interventions with the patience required in spiritual growth and development, as emphasized by C.S. Lewis's principle of putting first things first.
- **Miracles in the Process:** It is essential to recognize that while waiting for sudden breakthroughs, the gradual processes we undergo are also filled with smaller, yet significant, miracles that should be acknowledged and celebrated.

Conclusion

Chapter Twenty-Six captures the essence of divine 'suddenly' moments through the lens of Paul's transformative encounter on the road to Damascus.

It encourages believers to maintain a balance between expecting dramatic divine interventions and valuing the gradual processes of spiritual growth. This chapter invites readers to cultivate a readiness for God's unexpected actions while also engaging deeply in the ongoing journey of faith.

A SUMMARY OF THE ABSOLUTES

Bible Verse

"For I am convinced that neither death nor life, neither angels nor demons, neither the present nor the future, nor any powers, neither height nor depth, nor anything else in all creation, will be able to separate us from the love of God that is in Christ Jesus our Lord." - Romans 8:38-39 (NASB)

Introduction

This chapter compiles and reflects on the core beliefs and theological absolutes found in Paul's writings, emphasizing the certainty and lack of ambiguity in his declarations of faith. These absolutes, forged through his transformative encounter on the road to Damascus, offer a firm foundation for Christian belief and practice.

Word of Wisdom

"It feels almost heretical (but isn't) to say that Paul lived the New Testament before it was written." Paul Manwaring

Main Theme

The chapter focuses on the unwavering convictions derived from Paul's writings that define and solidify the essential truths of Christian faith. These theological absolutes not only guided Paul's ministry but continue to anchor modern Christian beliefs.

Key Points

- Paul's writings convey a series of absolute statements about faith, grace, and salvation, highlighting his unwavering certainty in God's promises.
- These absolutes include the effectiveness of God's grace, the inspiration of scripture, and the transformative power of being in Christ.
- Each statement is drawn from Paul's epistles and reflects significant theological pillars that are central to Christian doctrine.
- Paul's convictions provide a blueprint for understanding and navigating the Christian faith with clarity and confidence.
- These theological absolutes are intended to strengthen believers, providing a basis for faith and practice that counters doubt and bolsters spiritual courage.

Key Themes

- **The Role of Divine Providence in Paul's Theology:** Paul's assertion that "all things work together for good" encapsulates his belief in divine providence and reassures believers of God's omnipotent care in orchestrating life's circumstances for their spiritual benefit.
- **The Assurance of Salvation and Grace:** Key statements such as salvation through faith and the sufficiency of grace emphasize that Christian salvation is a gift from God, not earned by human effort, thus highlighting the foundational Protestant principle of 'sola fide' (faith alone).
- **The Unbreakable Bond with Christ:** The assertion that nothing can separate believers from the love of Christ reassures Christians of the eternal security and perpetual support available through their relationship with Jesus.
- **The Authority and Utility of Scripture:** Paul's declaration that "all Scripture is inspired" underscores the importance of the Bible in teaching, rebuking, correcting, and training in righteousness, serving as the ultimate guide for Christian living.
- **The New Identity in Christ:** The concept of believers as new creations in Christ reinforces the transformative effect of salvation, encouraging a break from past sins and a fresh start in spiritual life.

Conclusion

Chapter Twenty-Seven distills the essence of Paul's theological convictions into a series of unequivocal statements that collectively serve as a creed for Christian belief and practice. These absolutes, rooted in Paul's profound encounter with Christ, continue to inspire and stabilize the faith of believers, reminding them of the foundational truths upon which Christianity stands.

CHAPTER 28

ENCOUNTERS BECOME WEAPONS

Bible Verse

"For the kingdom of God is not in words, but in power." - 1 Corinthians 4:20 (NASB)

Introduction

Chapter Twenty-Eight explores how divine encounters, exemplified by Paul's Damascus road experience, transform into powerful testimonies and prophetic tools that shape personal faith and broader ministry impact. This chapter underscores the potency of these encounters in addressing and overcoming societal challenges.

Word of Wisdom

"Encounters are a vital part of that reset, equipping us for the needs and challenges of our day and for recalibrating our approach to life." Paul Manwaring

. . .

Main Theme

The transformative power of divine encounters serves as a foundational element for enduring faith and effective ministry, highlighting how personal experiences with God can become prophetic messages that address and influence both current and future societal conditions.

Key Points

- Paul used his dramatic conversion as a foundational testimony in his defense before King Agrippa, emphasizing the enduring impact of his encounter with Jesus.
- His transformation was so profound that it recalibrated his entire theological outlook and ministry approach.
- Paul's writings often reflect the solutions given to him during his encounter, which he applied to the societal issues of his time.
- These divine encounters provided Paul with both the message and the methodology to address complex problems within the church and society.
- The principles derived from Paul's experiences are timeless, offering relevant insights for addressing contemporary challenges.

Key Themes

- **Theological Transformation through Encounter:** Paul's encounter not only revolutionized his personal faith but also his theological directives, which he used to guide and instruct early Christian communities, particularly in complex environments like Corinth.
- **Prophetic Insight for Societal Application:** By reflecting on Paul's response to his divine encounter, the chapter illustrates how personal spiritual experiences can extend beyond individual transformation to address broad societal and cultural issues, offering divine solutions to human problems.
- **Enduring Relevance of Divine Encounters:** The timeless nature of the truths revealed in Paul's experiences demonstrates that encounters with God are not just for personal edification but are also intended to equip believers to effectively engage with the world.
- **Cultural and Moral Reflections:** Paul's application of his Damascus road encounter to the challenges of Corinth shows a profound understanding of cultural dynamics and the moral dilemmas of his time, which parallels many modern societal issues.
- **Empowerment for Contemporary Believers:** The chapter encourages modern believers to view their personal encounters with God as powerful tools for ministry and societal influence, urging

them to apply these divine insights to navigate and transform the current cultural landscape.

Conclusion

Chapter Twenty-Eight compellingly argues that personal encounters with the divine, such as Paul's conversion, are not isolated events but are meant to be leveraged as dynamic, transformative forces in the believer's life and ministry. These encounters are depicted as both weapons and tools, prophetic in nature, designed to confront and conquer both personal and societal challenges. The chapter calls believers to harness their spiritual experiences to impact the world effectively, drawing on Paul's example as a blueprint for integrating divine encounters with practical ministry and societal engagement.

CHAPTER 29

A LETTER TO THE CORINTHIANS

Bible Verse

"For the kingdom of God is not a matter of talk but of power." - 1 Corinthians 4:20 (NIV)

Introduction

Chapter Twenty-Nine dissects Paul's correspondence with the Corinthians, emphasizing how his divine encounter on the road to Damascus shaped his responses and teachings to a complex, cosmopolitan community struggling with cultural and spiritual issues similar to today's society.

Word of Wisdom

"Earth's wisdom wants an explanation; heaven's wisdom is a demonstration."
Paul Manwaring

Main Theme

The chapter presents Paul's letters to the Corinthians as not only responses to specific community challenges but as broader theological discourses deeply influenced by his transformative encounter with Christ, offering timeless wisdom applicable to contemporary issues.

Key Points

- Paul's approach to the Corinthians was shaped by his dramatic conversion, emphasizing wisdom, knowledge, and the power of the Spirit.
- His letters tackle deep-rooted issues within the Corinthian church, reflecting conflicts between heavenly wisdom and earthly wisdom.
- Paul contrasts the fleeting wisdom of the age with the profound, seemingly foolish wisdom from God.
- He uses his own transformation as a testament to the power of divine wisdom over human knowledge.
- Paul's writings to Corinth remain relevant, addressing modern-day challenges such as information overload, cultural shifts, and the integrity of faith.

Key Themes

- **Transformation Through Divine Wisdom:** Paul's foundational experience with Christ's power profoundly shaped his theological outlook, emphasizing that true wisdom often appears foolish to the world but holds the key to deep spiritual insights and solutions.

- **Addressing Societal Complexities with Heavenly Insights:** By focusing on the transformation wrought by heavenly wisdom, Paul's letters provide a blueprint for navigating the complexities of modern cultural and spiritual landscapes, advocating for a focus on divine rather than human wisdom.
- **The Relevance of Pauline Epistles to Modern Challenges:** The issues faced by the Corinthian church, such as division, immorality, and the pursuit of status, mirror today's societal problems, making Paul's guidance as pertinent now as it was then.
- **Counteracting Earthly Wisdom with Spiritual Truths:** Paul challenges believers to rethink their adherence to worldly wisdom by presenting the supremacy of spiritual knowledge that leads to true understanding and relationship with God.
- **The Enduring Power of Testimony:** Paul leverages his personal encounter with Jesus as a continuous source of authority and inspiration, illustrating how personal testimonies can serve as powerful tools in ministry and personal growth.

Conclusion

Chapter Twenty-Nine elucidates how Paul's epistles to the Corinthians, derived from his life-changing encounter with Jesus, offer profound insights into dealing with internal church conflicts and societal issues through divine wisdom. This chapter encourages readers to apply Paul's teachings to overcome modern challenges by embracing heavenly wisdom over earthly knowledge, fostering a deeper relationship with God through authentic spiritual experiences.

CHAPTER 30

THE APPLICATION OF SAUL'S ENCOUNTER IN CORINTH AND PRESENT DAY

Bible Verse

"Do you not know that your body is a temple of the Holy Spirit within you, whom you have from God? You are not your own." - 1 Corinthians 6:19 (ESV)

Introduction

In this chapter, the profound impact of Paul's transformative encounter with Jesus on the road to Damascus is explored through its application to the issues faced by the Corinthian church, revealing its relevance to contemporary challenges in our own "modern-day Corinth."

Word of Wisdom

"An encounter will cause us to walk differently." Paul Manwaring

Main Theme

Paul's responses to various issues within the Corinthian church, rooted in his dramatic encounter with Jesus, offer timeless solutions that resonate with challenges faced by today's church and society.

Key Points

- Paul addresses fifteen areas of correction within the Corinthian church, each applicable to contemporary church and societal issues.
- His guidance is deeply influenced by his conversion experience, emphasizing transformation and redemption.
- Paul's focus is on internal church reform rather than societal moral judgment.
- The teachings on immorality stress the identity of believers as temples of the Holy Spirit.
- Paul's solutions to church issues always circle back to understanding and embodying the character of Christ.

Key Themes

- **Transformation Through Divine Encounter:** Paul's teachings on overcoming immorality focus on the believer's identity as a temple of the Holy Spirit, influenced by his own transformation from persecutor to apostle. His guidance advocates for a life of purity inspired by love and honor for

Christ, rather than through legalistic adherence.

- **Addressing Church vs. Societal Issues:** While Paul's letters to the Corinthians address misconduct within the church, he distinctly avoids casting judgment on external societal behaviors. This highlights his strategy of strengthening the church's moral foundation to influence broader cultural change.

- **Comprehensive Solutions Rooted in Personal Change:** Each correction Paul offers is not merely about behavior modification but involves a deep, personal transformation reflecting his own life-changing encounter with Jesus. His solutions emphasize the believer's new identity in Christ and the consequent behavioral changes.

- **The Role of Personal Testimony in Teaching:** Paul uses his own dramatic testimony not only as a credential but as a powerful teaching tool to illustrate the life-changing power of an encounter with Christ. His personal change underscores every instruction and correction he offers to the Corinthians.

- **Ongoing Relevance of Pauline Instructions:** The issues Paul addressed —ranging from immorality to disputes within the church—are mirrored in today's church challenges, making his apostolic wisdom and solutions perpetually relevant and necessary for contemporary Christian life and governance.

Conclusion

Chapter Thirty elucidates how Paul's encounter with Christ on the road to Damascus is not just a foundational moment for his ministry but serves as a blueprint for dealing with issues within the church throughout ages. His transformative experience offers profound lessons on handling challenges that transcend time, urging modern believers to reflect on their spiritual encounters and apply these insights to navigate their own "Corinthian" complexities with grace and wisdom.

CHAPTER 31

ENCOUNTERS FOR ALL

Bible Verse

"For since the creation of the world God's invisible qualities—his eternal power and divine nature—have been clearly seen, being understood from what has been made, so that people are without excuse." — Romans 1:20 (NIV)

Introduction

This chapter challenges the cessationist view that supernatural encounters with God ceased with the apostles, arguing that such experiences are accessible to all believers, not just historical figures. The author asserts that theology should lead to Kingdom behavior that reflects God's ongoing presence and power.

Word of Wisdom

"If our theology does not produce Kingdom behavior, which points to the

Father, then I suggest that we review our theology, not seek or argue to change the nature, attributes, and power of God."
Paul Manwaring

Main Theme

The chapter emphasizes the universal availability of divine encounters, arguing against the notion that miraculous experiences ended with the apostles. It suggests that the true purpose of theology is to facilitate ongoing personal experiences with God, reflecting His enduring power and presence.

Key Points

- Supernatural encounters did not cease with the apostles but are accessible to all believers today.
- Theology should be about discovering and applying God's truths in a way that encourages personal encounters with Him.
- Not all teachings branded as theological reflect true Christian doctrine, particularly when they deny God's ongoing miraculous works.
- Personal encounters with God are diverse and can manifest in dramatic, supernatural events or through simple, daily interactions.
- Encounters with God cultivate a deeper personal faith and a communal expectation of ongoing divine interaction.

- Creating a culture that expects and cherishes divine encounters is crucial for the vibrancy and growth of Christian faith.

Key Themes

- **The Nature of Theological Teachings:** The author critiques teachings that limit or deny the supernatural aspects of God's interaction with humanity, labeling such teachings as untheological and unbiblical. He stresses that true theology should facilitate an experiential knowledge of God, drawing individuals and communities closer to Him.
- **Encounters Across the Spectrum:** Encounters with God are presented as varied and personalized—ranging from dramatic visions to quiet moments of inspiration. These encounters are not reserved for the biblical era but are meant for all believers, emphasizing that God actively seeks to engage with His followers in myriad ways.
- **Cultural Shifts in Perception:** The chapter discusses the need to shift church culture from viewing divine encounters as rare or historical to seeing them as daily, accessible, and essential to Christian living. This cultural shift helps believers to remain open to experiencing God in their everyday lives.
- **Implications of a Limited Theology:** The author warns against a theology that limits God's power or works, suggesting that such a perspective can stunt spiritual

growth and diminish the richness of a believer's personal relationship with God.

- **The Role of Community and Culture in Spiritual Encounters:** By fostering a community that actively pursues and values divine encounters, believers can create an environment where spiritual growth is nurtured, and the reality of God's power is continually witnessed.

- **Practical Steps to Cultivate Encounter:** The text provides practical advice on how to cultivate a lifestyle that is open to divine encounters, such as through prayer, meditation on Scripture, communal worship, and maintaining a heart of expectancy.

Conclusion

"Encounters for All" serves as a powerful reminder that encounters with the divine are not relics of the past but vibrant, essential aspects of contemporary Christian life. By embracing a theology that acknowledges and seeks out God's manifest presence, believers can experience a faith that is alive and transformative. The author's message encourages a reevaluation of personal and communal theological frameworks to ensure they promote a direct, on-going experience with God, fostering a richer, more dynamic faith journey.

CHAPTER 32

OUR ENCOUNTERS

Bible Verse

"But rise and stand on your feet; for I have appeared to you for this purpose, to make you a minister and a witness both of the things which you have seen and of the things which I will yet reveal to you." — Acts 26:16 (NKJV)

Introduction

In this chapter, the author explores the transformative power of encounters with God, drawing parallels between Saul's encounter on the road to Damascus and our own spiritual experiences. The chapter emphasizes the importance of recording, reflecting on, and responding to these encounters as part of a larger journey toward personal transformation and fulfilling one's destiny.

Word of Wisdom

"Encounters change us. They bring transformation—for us and for the world

in which we have influence." Paul Manwaring

Main Theme

Our encounters with God are invitations to live differently, equipping us with the strength and insight needed for spiritual growth and impact. These encounters present us with choices and responsibilities, requiring us to steward them well in order to maximize their effect on our lives and the lives of those around us.

Key Points

- Encounters are opportunities to transform both ourselves and the world around us.
- Saul's encounter serves as a model for how transformative divine moments can be.
- Each encounter gives us a choice to embrace or reject the change it offers.
- Reflecting on our encounters strengthens us and prepares us for future ones.
- Encounters involve both our action and God's intervention to bring about their full impact.
- The Encounter Audit is a tool to assess and maximize the significance of spiritual experiences.

Key Themes

- **Encounters Offer Transformation:**
- Just as Saul's encounter on the road to Damascus radically transformed his life,

our spiritual encounters have the power to change the course of our lives. These encounters shift not only our personal outlook but also empower us to influence others and shape the world around us.

- **Choice and Responsibility in Encounters:**
- Encounters come with choices—whether to accept the changes they prompt or to resist them. The chapter stresses that encounters are not passive events; they require our active participation to see the transformation fulfilled.
- **Encounters and Prophetic Culture:**
- Encounters often align with prophetic words and guidance, but they thrive in a culture that values and nurtures such experiences. By creating an environment that honors encounters, we position ourselves to see God's purposes come to fruition in our lives.
- **Divine and Human Partnership in Encounters:**
- The author outlines that encounters have both human and divine elements. We are called to act on what we can, while leaving space for God's supernatural intervention to complete what only He can do.
- **Reflecting on Encounters for Future Growth:**
- Reflecting on past encounters is essential for spiritual growth. The Encounter Audit helps to process these experiences and extract lessons that can guide us in future decisions, allowing each encounter to become a building block for the next.

Conclusion

Our encounters with God are life-changing moments that equip us for greater influence and growth. They present us with choices, requiring both our action and God's intervention to reach their full potential. By reflecting on these encounters and stewarding them well, we allow them to shape our personal lives, ministries, and relationship with God in profound ways. Encounters are not just emotional experiences; they are invitations to step into our destiny and serve others.

CHAPTER 33

THE BATTLE IS THE LORD'S

Bible Verse

"For the battle is not yours, but God's." — 2 Chronicles 20:15 (NASB)

Introduction

This chapter delves into the concept of how believers should live and respond to challenges after encountering God. Using Saul's conversion and Gamaliel's wisdom from the Book of Acts as foundational examples, the chapter emphasizes the importance of recognizing when God is fighting for us and resisting the urge to fight in our own strength. It challenges readers to allow God to lead in battles, while taking responsibility for what we can control.

Word of Wisdom

"One of the challenges and opportunities of the Christian life is to identify

where God is fighting for us and then let Him win." Paul Manwaring

Main Theme

The battle belongs to the Lord, and we must learn to discern when God is fighting on our behalf. Instead of resisting or fighting against God's plan, believers are called to cooperate with His divine strategy, recognizing that while battles occur, the victory is ultimately His.

Key Points

- Saul's encounter on the road to Damascus highlights the necessity of yielding to God's leading.
- Gamaliel's wisdom reminds us not to fight against God's plans, as they will ultimately succeed.
- In moments of trial, we must choose whether to trust in God's victory or to resist in our strength.
- Our responses to life's challenges should be rooted in recognizing God's active role in our battles.
- Denying responsibility or blaming others prevents spiritual growth and blocks God's intervention.
- Spiritual discernment helps us recognize when we are facing a divine battle and encourages us to stand firm in faith.

Key Themes

YIELDING TO GOD'S PLAN:

- Gamaliel's advice to the Sanhedrin—to avoid fighting against what might be a work of God—serves as a powerful reminder for believers. We must learn to discern when God is moving in our lives and trust His plan, even when it challenges our personal agendas.

THE IMPORTANCE OF DISCERNMENT:

- Not every trial or battle is meant to be fought with human effort. Discernment is crucial in identifying when to stand still and let God fight for us, and when to take action in partnership with His leading. Understanding the spiritual significance of battles allows us to navigate them wisely.

OWNERSHIP AND GROWTH:

- Taking responsibility for our part in the battles we face is essential for spiritual maturity. Blaming others or refusing to acknowledge personal responsibility can hinder repentance and stunt growth, preventing us from fully benefiting from the lessons God intends to teach.

TRUSTING GOD IN THE MIDST OF BATTLE:

- The Christian life is filled with conflicts, but not all require physical or emotional struggle. Learning to trust that God fights for us, especially in unseen spiritual battles, enables us to experience peace even in the midst of trials.

FIGHTING THE GOOD FIGHT:

- Paul's charge to "fight the good fight" highlights that not all battles are worth engaging in. A good fight is one where God is leading, and we align with His purposes. Knowing which battles to engage in and which to leave to God is key to living victoriously.

Conclusion

The battle is indeed the Lord's, but believers must be wise in recognizing their role in the conflicts they face. Whether through discernment, repentance, or standing firm in faith, we are called to cooperate with God's strategy rather than fighting against Him. In every battle, God's victory is assured when we allow Him to lead and stand in alignment with His will.

CHAPTER 34

A CHALLENGE

Bible Verse

"For I am not ashamed of the gospel of Christ, for it is the power of God to salvation for everyone who believes." —
Romans 1:16 (NKJV)

Introduction

As the journey draws to a close, the author presents a challenge to embrace five key principles rooted in the simplicity and purity of the gospel. Inspired by Paul's transformative encounter on the road to Damascus, these principles—power, presence, salvation, communion, and ambassadorship—serve as the foundation for a life of ministry and purpose. Each principle represents a core focus from which all other expressions of faith should flow, empowering believers to live fully in the gospel's truth.

Word of Wisdom

"My challenge is that you embrace five principles and priorities in your life and ministry." Paul Manwaring

Main Theme

This chapter challenges believers to focus on five core principles—power, presence, salvation, communion, and ambassadorship—as the foundation for living out the gospel. By adhering to these principles, we can experience the fullness of God's purpose in our lives and effectively share the Good News with others.

Key Points

- Demonstrating God's power should be central to our lives, showing His intervention and presence.
- Recognizing that we are temples of the Holy Spirit helps prevent division and moral failure.
- Salvation and the resurrection of Jesus must be proclaimed with unwavering faith.
- Communion fosters fellowship, unity, and the remembrance of Christ's sacrifice.
- Every believer is an ambassador, sent to bring reconciliation and represent Jesus in the world.

Key Themes

- Paul emphasized that the power of God must be demonstrated, not merely spoken about. Signs, wonders, and miracles are integral to the simplicity of the Christian faith, even when they require perseverance and faith to manifest.

- Recognizing that we are temples of the Holy Spirit reshapes our identity and ministry. This understanding prevents moral failures, discourages division based on leadership, and promotes a deep sense of unity as we all carry the same divine presence.

- The resurrected Jesus was central to Paul's ministry, and it must be central to ours as well. Denying the resurrection undermines the gospel, but proclaiming it offers hope, salvation, and the ultimate answer to deconstruction and denial of faith.

- Communion is a vital act of worship that fosters fellowship and unity among believers. It reminds us of Christ's sacrifice and strengthens our relationships, emphasizing that we were created for community and shared spiritual experiences.

- Every believer is sent with a mission, carrying the authority and responsibility to represent Christ. As ambassadors of reconciliation, we are called to restore what is broken and bring heaven's influence into the world, fulfilling our divine assignment.

Conclusion

The challenge in this chapter is clear: embrace these five principles—power, presence, salvation, communion, and ambassadorship—as the foundation of your life and ministry. By doing so, you will not only live out the simplicity and purity of the gospel but also lead others to encounter the transformative power of Christ.

CHAPTER 35

COUNTERING THE NARRATIVES OF OUR WORLD

Bible Verse

"For the weapons of our warfare are not carnal but mighty in God for pulling down strongholds, casting down arguments and every high thing that exalts itself against the knowledge of God." — 2 Corinthians 10:4-5 (NKJV)

Introduction

In a world dominated by powerful cultural narratives, believers are constantly bombarded by distorted versions of truth that shape their perspectives. This chapter addresses how Christians can recognize and counter these narratives by understanding them through the lens of biblical truth. By rooting our worldview in God's Word, we can dismantle the strongholds these narratives create and embrace a life that reflects heaven's perspective.

Word of Wisdom

"Our faith, the history of our faith, and the lessons of Paul teach us to bombard the worldview with our heaven view."
Paul Manwaring

Main Theme

The world presents many distorted narratives that subtly erode Christian values and perspectives. Believers are called to counter these narratives by renewing their minds with God's truth and ensuring that their theology is based on encounters with God rather than academic knowledge alone.

Key Points

- Eight prominent cultural narratives—such as consumerism and moral relativism—distort truth and shape modern worldviews.
- These cultural strongholds must be countered through the knowledge of God and spiritual discernment.
- Carrying God's Word and presence with us helps us resist the desensitizing effects of these narratives.
- Theology must be rooted in a relationship with God, not merely academic study.
- Paul's "task theology" emphasizes living out our faith in daily life through encounters with Christ.

- Knowledge alone can lead to arrogance, but being known by God leads to humility and love.

Key Themes

- The modern world is filled with pervasive narratives, like consumerism and individualism, which present twisted versions of truth. These narratives subtly shape our thinking, and we must be aware of how they impact our worldview and spiritual life.
- Scot McKnight's list of cultural strongholds reminds us that the battle is not just physical or dramatic but often subtle and daily. Christians are called to counter these false narratives by immersing themselves in Scripture and renewing their minds with the knowledge of God.
- The chapter stresses the difference between lived theology—faith applied in everyday life—and academic theology, which can sometimes be detached from real-world application. Paul's approach to theology was practical, rooted in his personal encounters with Christ, and this should guide how we engage with theological study.
- Paul's transformation on the road to Damascus is a key example of how encounters with God shape our theology. Our understanding of God must be grounded in relational knowledge, not just intellectual understanding. This lived

encounter changes how we think, act, and interact with the world.

- Paul emphasizes that love, not knowledge, is what builds up. While knowledge is valuable, it can lead to pride if disconnected from love and relationship with God. True theology must always serve to deepen our relationship with the Father, Son, and Holy Spirit, leading to transformation.

Conclusion

To counter the strongholds of the world's distorted narratives, Christians must engage in the "task theology" of daily life, rooted in real encounters with God. This requires a conscious effort to live out our theology in practice, allowing God's truth to shape our worldview and dismantle the false narratives that surround us. As we prioritize our relationship with God over mere knowledge, we are empowered to stand firm in faith and bring heaven's perspective to earth.

CHAPTER 36

TRANSFORMATION BY ENCOUNTER

Bible Verse

"But we all, with unveiled face, beholding as in a mirror the glory of the Lord, are being transformed into the same image from glory to glory, just as by the Spirit of the Lord." — 2 Corinthians 3:18 (NKJV)

Introduction

In this chapter, Bill Johnson explores the profound impact that encounters with God have on a believer's life. These experiences are not just emotional or spiritual moments, but deeply transformative encounters that change us at our core. Drawing examples from the Bible, Johnson illustrates how divine encounters, such as those of Paul and Peter, bring about radical personal and communal transformation. The chapter challenges readers to seek such encounters and allow the presence of God to continually shape their lives.

Word of Wisdom

"God experiences are transformative in nature. The lesser is always affected by the greater." Bill Johnson

Main Theme

Encounters with God have the power to radically transform our lives, aligning us with His will and likeness. These experiences draw us closer to Him and impart His presence, which changes our character, empowers us for ministry, and sanctifies us.

Key Points

- Encounters with God lead to personal transformation, as seen in the life of the apostle Paul.
- Divine virtue is imparted during encounters, bringing healing and restoration.
- Peter's transformation on the Day of Pentecost illustrates the power of the Holy Spirit to change hearts.
- Beholding God in His glory transforms us into His image.
- Every encounter with God, whether dramatic or subtle, invites us to deeper intimacy and faith.

Key Themes

- Encounters with God are not just isolated spiritual experiences, but moments that leave a lasting imprint on the individual. As Paul and Peter's lives were radically transformed by their encounters with Christ, so too are we changed when we encounter His presence.

- Johnson emphasizes that divine encounters impart the very presence of God into our lives. Like the woman who touched Jesus' garment and was healed, when we touch or encounter God, His virtue—the power of the Holy Spirit—is imparted, bringing transformation.

- To behold God is to be changed by Him. As believers turn their hearts to focus on God's glory, they are transformed from within. This transformation is not merely behavioral but reflects a deep, internal change that aligns us with His nature and character.

- Holiness, or becoming more like God, is achieved through encounters with Him. Sanctification is a process where we are continually separated from the things that defile us and drawn closer to God's purposes, ultimately reflecting His holiness in our lives.

- While some encounters with God are overwhelming, others are quieter, marked by His silence. Johnson reminds readers that even in these moments, God is leading us back to what He has already spoken, teaching us to walk in faith based on the strength of previous encounters.

Conclusion

Encounters with God, whether powerful or subtle, are transformative and life-giving. They enable us to experience His presence, receive His virtue, and grow in holiness. As we seek God's face, we are changed into His image, empowered to fulfill our calling, and strengthened to walk by faith even in seasons of silence. Through continual encounters, we live a life that reflects the glory and goodness of God.

CHAPTER 37

OUR FUTURE ENCOUNTERS

Bible Verse

"Behold, I stand at the door and knock. If anyone hears My voice and opens the door, I will come in to him and dine with him, and he with Me." — Revelation 3:20 (NKJV)

Introduction

This chapter focuses on the importance of future encounters with God, emphasizing that such experiences are not only possible but necessary for spiritual growth. Encounters with God are meant to transform us and propel us into the fullness of our calling in Christ. Paul's life is used as a model to show how one encounter can shape and influence an entire lifetime of ministry, urging readers to continually pursue more encounters with God as a means of personal transformation and societal impact.

Word of Wisdom

"Our encounters are the beginning, not the end; the foundation, not the goal; the source of our future direction, passion, momentum, and purity." Paul Manwaring

Main Theme

Encounters with God are designed to continually transform us, and they are foundational for living out our Christian calling. These experiences allow us to grow into the fullness of Christ, equipping us to carry out His purpose in the world.

Key Points

Encounters with God are transformative and make us whole in Christ, just as Paul's encounter completed his understanding of scripture and calling.

We are invited to continually pursue encounters with God, seeking His presence in our lives.

Reading the Bible through the lens of encounters reveals how God uses ordinary people to fulfill extraordinary purposes.

Encounters shape our sense of calling, propelling us into the mission God has set before us.

Paul's encounter with Jesus serves as an example of deep, personal transformation that extended to the broader world.

These encounters prepare us for our future, giving us the tools to fight for our destiny and purpose.

Key Themes

- The Bible is filled with invitations for us to seek more encounters with God. These encounters are not just one-time events but should be an ongoing pursuit in our Christian walk, as they are essential for deeper intimacy with God and spiritual growth.
- The Bible should be read as a collection of divine encounters where God touched and transformed the lives of ordinary men and women. Through these stories, we are encouraged to believe that similar encounters are possible for us today.
- Like Paul, who was transformed by his encounter with Jesus on the road to Damascus, our encounters with God reveal and affirm our calling. These moments give us clarity and direction for our mission in life and provide the power to fulfill it.
- The current generation, marked by division and protest, is in desperate need of a divine interruption. Just as Paul's encounter brought radical transformation, the author suggests that God's power can intervene in our time to unite and revive a generation.
- Encounters with God are not just personal experiences; they become our testimonies and prophetic tools. These encounters strengthen us to fight for our destiny, shaping our character and empowering us to influence the world for God's kingdom.

Conclusion

Encounters with God are not just isolated experiences but are meant to guide and prepare us for the future. As we continue to pursue these encounters, we are shaped into the image of Christ, empowered for our calling, and equipped to impact the world around us. By looking to biblical examples like Paul, we can see the transformative power of divine encounters and trust that our own experiences with God are preparing us for a destiny filled with purpose and influence.

※

◗ DESTINY IMAGE

Destiny Image is a prophetic Christian publisher dedicated to empowering believers through Spirit-led messages. Our mission is to equip and inspire individuals to fulfill their God-given destinies by providing transformative resources that resonate with the Charismatic and Pentecostal faith.

We specialize in books, blogs, and back cover copies that reflect prophetic insights, dynamic teachings, and testimonies of faith. Our commitment to fostering spiritual growth and kingdom impact makes Destiny Image a beacon for those seeking to deepen their relationship with God and embrace their calling in the power of the Holy Spirit.